TURNING THINGS UPSIDE DOWN

TURNING THINGS UPSIDE DOWN

A Theological Workbook

THOMAS B. WOODWARD

A CROSSROAD BOOK   THE SEABURY PRESS · NEW YORK

Copyright © 1975 by The Seabury Press, Inc.
Designed by Carol Basen
Printed in the United States of America.

LIBRARY OF CONGRESS CATALOGING IN PUBLICATION DATA

Woodward, Thomas B.   1937-
   Turning things upside down.

   "A Crossroad book."
   1. Christian life—1960-   2. Church.
I. Title.
BV4501.2.W64   248'.4   74-31439
ISBN 0-8164-0279-5

For Judy, my wife,
and Tommy, Jenny, and
Joy our children.

*In praise of their
beauty and light.*

Contents

Acknowledgments

I wish to thank Bob Gilday of The Seabury Press for his early encouragement and on-going support in the writing of this book.

I want to thank, also, Doris Van Vechten and the Board for Campus Ministry (not a rock band, but my employing agency) for giving me the time to spend in putting this book together. It is a rare employer that sees writing as part of the on-going ministry of the Church—and I am fortunate enough to have such a Board.

My colleagues in campus ministry at the University of Rochester have been most helpful in checking out many of my less than orthodox ideas, either pulling me back toward reason or encouraging me in my heterodoxy. My deep appreciation to them: Paul Walaskay for his help on biblical exegesis, Rabbi Joseph Levine for his helpful and thoughtful assistance in dealing with Jewish life and thought, Joan Sobala, Frank Snow, and Jim Lawlor for their constant insight and encouragement.

Of special help throughout has been Lavonne Swearingen, secretary, critic, and friend. Time after time she provided the critical phrase, helped delete the patent nonsense, and played the important role of devil's advocate.

And lastly, I wish to acknowledge my great debt to my father, Webb, who died this past year. It was for him that I began to write this book and whatever good comes from its publication redounds to the beauty of his life.

TURNING THINGS UPSIDE DOWN

1

Before You Begin

Perhaps the best way to introduce what follows is for me to relate an incident in my own life. It took place at a workshop on "The Bible for Youth and Adults" led by Reuven Gold, a "professional storyteller."

Soon after the workshop had begun, a newly ordained minister pleaded his own predicament, "About ten minutes after I begin teaching my fifth grade Bible class there is absolute chaos in the classroom. And I don't know what to do."

Reuven responded quietly, "What *kind* of chaos?"

"What do you mean 'What kind of chaos'—it's just chaos; plain, simple, unmitigated chaos!"

"Well," said Reuven, "there are several kinds of chaos."

"I don't get it," the young man replied. "I don't know how it happens, whether it's something I do or they do, but ten minutes after we begin it's chaos—and I don't know what to do!"

Reuven thought for a minute, put his finger to his chin, and responded, "This may not be of immediate help to you, but then again it might. The Lord created the heavens and the earth from chaos and void, so never neglect it as a resource."

Part of what I have tried to do in this book is to uncover the chaotic in the Christian faith. I have made no effort to be consistent or systematic in moving from issue to issue or theme to theme. Rather, just the opposite: I have made every effort to be contradictory and suggestive when things could have been laid out neatly and in order.

I have always been suspicious of books that have everything carefully tied down in precise, logical, and thematic consistency. Life, as I know it, just isn't that way, nor is the Christian faith as lived and experienced through the ages. So nothing is "packaged" here. If you want a nice, neat Christmas package, this is not the place to look.

Most people of the Western world are uncomfortable with contradiction. We love to synthesize, to bring everything into nice, neat wholes. But in doing so we often do violence to the dialectical parts. To combine and synthesize separate realities too soon is to rob them of their power. To illustrate:

> Jesus was a marvellous, thoroughly delightful clown—even to the end.
>
> Jesus sensed the urgency and the seriousness of his mission early in his public life. "The shadow of the Cross fell over his whole ministry," to coin a phrase.

Both these appraisals are apt: both themes run all the way through the gospel record. But they cannot be brought together into a single, consistent understanding of Jesus ("In pressing on toward Jerusalem, we often see Jesus making use of his wonderful sense of humor").

It is only an insecure or adolescent kind of logic that will not allow us to believe at least two contradictory things as true. If scientists can get along with their mutually exclusive theories of light, why can't theologians be as generous?

> So beware of synthesists in sheep's clothing. They are out to rob you of the richness of multiple and contradictory truths.

What I am trying to do in this book is to open up the Christian faith so ordinary people can begin to relate to it in a more personal and open way. I am trying to create the kind of climate where we can ask the right questions and begin to find the sorts of answers which are true both to our own deeper selves and to the biblical tradition.

Thus, it is important to me to be suggestive, rather than definitive (there are plenty of definitive books on the Christian faith—some very good and many that are simply atrocious). I am conscious of how very, very much is left unsaid in every chapter. But again, completeness or comprehensiveness (in the narrow sense) are not what I am after.

As a more definite indication of what to expect, in the chapter on the Church, I have attempted to introduce three distinct "feelings" or traditions about the Church. Each is, in some sense, true and faithful to tradition. But to take any one of these three views seriously means that you will have trouble with at least one of the other two. Thus the subtitle, "A Theological Workbook." That is fair warning that you are not expected to read this material passively. My fondest wish is that you will find yourself engaged in a wrestling match and in that process discover that doing theology is both fun and exciting.

Originally, I had proposed a different title: "An Outrageous

Book." I did this partly to share in the delight of walking into a bookstore to begin an impromptu Abbott and Costello routine by saying, "I would like to buy 'An Outrageous Book,'" and partly because the book is full of outrageous kinds of theology. But however outrageous some of my material seems to be, I stand by almost all of it (to disclose the frivolous or the put-on would be to destroy the Workbook before you begin).

Outside of this introduction I have rigorously attempted to avoid pronouncements. In fact, this may be the only book published this year where all pronouncements are clearly labelled! I apologize in advance for any I have failed to label.

The Christian life is an exciting, absorbing, and often risky sort of existence. I very much enjoy trying to communicate that. But, again, it is difficult to speak of Christianity in any neat, clear, straightforward way. I am aware that people have attempted to do just that, with precise outlines of how this follows that and with lists of definite questions followed by even more definite answers. But always the effort is a disaster. Learning the Christian faith must not be made like learning multiplication tables, for the Christian faith is not like a multiplication table: it is open-ended and full of life. It speaks of profound realities and rejoices in paradox and seeming contradiction. This it does with no trace of shame or embarrassment—but with a certain glee.

> As the Hasidic saying goes: A man must have two pockets into which he can reach at one time or another, depending on his need. In his right pocket he must keep the words, "For my sake was the world created." And in his left, "I am but dust and ashes."

Thus it is with the complicated business life is. And it is in this spirit that the following is offered.

2
A Good Place
to Begin

A short while ago I saw an advertisement by a group of people offering a special edition of the Bible. Supposedly, all the objectionable material had been taken out. All the stories of rape, violence, adultery, murder, and the like were censored. What had been an X-rated book had suddenly become Family Entertainment!

If you've read your Bible, you know what they're talking about: the Song of Songs contains more eroticism than four of the best from Grove Press. And parts of Ezekiel make the Song of Songs read like *The Readers' Digest*.

In the Episcopal Church (that Church from which I come), we "censor" much of the Bible. Even some of the Psalms are too offensive for public reading, not to mention such undesirable characters as Ohaliah, Gomar, and Jezebel. And so we try to ignore the material that offends us.

And we all practice another kind of censorship of the Bible. Perhaps it is because we don't want to look at things as they really are. Why else would we picture Jesus in such incredibly long, flowing robes. (If he ever really tried to take a step in them he would surely fall over, flat on his face.) Notice that his robes are never dirty. No wine or breakfast is ever spilled on them. And his nails are always well manicured. We might call this "Antiseptic Religion."

Whenever we fail to take the Bible seriously, we always end up with antiseptic religion. Look at the way the Bible *does* portray Jesus. We find him drinking wine with his friends, hot and dirty, angry, disappointed, and sometimes even pretty violent—but never, *never* sickly sweet! There are a lot of ways to censor the Bible.

In hopes of bucking this trend of censorship, we ought to begin near the beginning by dealing with one of the "Bad Guys of the Bible." Near the beginning of Biblical history, God was telling

Moses what to say to the Hebrew slaves who were yearning for their freedom:

> Say this to the people of Israel,
> "The God of your fathers,
> The God of Abraham, the God of Isaac, and the God of Jacob,
> has sent me to you . . ."

"The God of Jacob." That sneaks by so neatly, so quickly that few people ever register the appropriate shock.

If *anything* in the Bible is to be glossed over to protect our sense of good taste, this is the place to start. Except for the Cross of Jesus, nothing could be more offensive. "The God of Jacob." Think back for a moment to what you know of Jacob. I dare you to find one person in the Old Testament who is more detestable than Jacob! That's right. I challenge you to find one person in the *whole* of the Bible more detestable than Jacob:

> Adam was peanuts compared to Jacob.
> Cain slew his brother: Jacob kept Esau alive to torment him
> for a lifetime.
> Jezebel was wicked enough, but beside Jacob she looks
> saintly.

Take a look at his life of crime:

> He cheated his brother out of his birthright for a bowl of soup.
> He stole his father-in-law blind.
> He had children by four women—by his two wives and each
> of their maids.
> By taking advantage of his nearly blind father,
> he stole his brother's inheritance.
> He had a knock-down, drag-out fight with an angel.
> He tried to bribe God.
> In fact, if you remember, Jacob's life of crime and deceit
> began even before he had left his mother's womb!

In short, Jacob was a thieving, cowardly, deceitful, blasphemous, ungrateful, polygamous, cheating, lying, dirty, old scoundrel. If you ever teach a Sunday School class and find you need examples of breaking the Ten Commandments, look no further—Jacob broke them all, in grand style.

Jacob's life was not clean, reverent, trustworthy, brave, loyal, obedient or any other characteristic of a modern day Boy Scout;

yet we continue to embarrass ourselves by saying, in one Psalm,

"Shout for joy to the God of Jacob" —PSALM 81.1

And if all this were not offensive enough, God renamed Jacob, "Israel." Jacob, the biggest scoundrel the Bible has ever known —Jacob was to be the father of the Jewish nation. And the Christian Church does not trace its history from Pentecost. It stretches back to Jacob himself. So if we are to censor our Bible, we ought to begin with this most offensive of all phrases: "The God of Jacob." It is of obvious embarrassment: if not to us, then surely to God.

But strangely enough, while Jacob seems to be the shame of our tradition, he also represents much of its glory. If we take this phrase, "The God of Jacob," at all seriously, we are forced to realize one very important thing: God is powerful enough to step into *any* life and work great things through it. To put it another way, God works not only through the saints, but also through the backsliders of the world.

This is really kind of amazing. God worked through Jacob, probably the most miserable sinner in the Bible. God not only worked through Jacob—*He named his people after him*!

What a crazy thing to do. What an incredibly bad joke! But that is what happened. And that is what *is* happening. God is reaching right down into real history, touching our incomplete lives and using them for good. That is the way God works: coming to us, loving us, beginning with us where we are. So maybe it is not so odd that Jacob was renamed, "Israel."

The God of Jacob is *not* a God of those who are worthy to serve him. Jesus, after all, made this so very clear in his own life. His closest friends were not particularly pleasant people, nor was a single one worthy of his friendship. In fact, might that not be the whole point of their calling? Of our calling?

I don't know anyone who has seen this more clearly than Holden Caulfield, a character in J. D. Salinger's book, *The Catcher in the Rye*. Complaining that he feels unable to pray, he says:

> "I can't always pray when I feel like it. In the first place, I'm sort of an atheist. I like Jesus and all, but I don't care too much for most of the other stuff in the Bible.
> Take the Disciples, for instance. They annoy the hell out of me, if you want to know the truth . . . They were all right after Jesus was dead and all, but while He was alive, they were about as much use to him as a hole in the head.

All they did was keep letting him down. I like almost anybody in the Bible better than the Disciples."[1]

But people like the disciples are *just* the people whom God has called to be part of his kingdom, to carry his name. *These* are the sort of people who carry on God's work in the world . . . people like you and me. The Jacobs. No matter how mixed up, or shattered, or shameful our lives, he is still our God. *If he can stick it out with Jacob, he can stick it out with us!*

It seems to me that far from an embarrassment, Jacob stands as a symbol of our hope. The God who rules over heaven and earth and countless galaxies cares for Jacob, loves Jacob, and calls him to be a son.

In one of the "forgotten parables," a vineyard owner sees a worthless fig tree and, much like a "god of the worthy" who sweeps away everyone who doesn't measure up, he asks his foreman to clear it out: "Year after year I have come looking for fruit from this fig tree, and I am always disappointed. Cut it down. Why should it use up the ground?"

But the foreman pleads for the plant: "Let it be. I'll dig around it, fertilize it, love it. Then we'll see." (Luke 13:6-9)

That is the God of Jacob—and the God of our Lord, Jesus Christ.

You and I, standing before the Father, gather up all our failures, all our incredible failures and offer them to him. Hardly worthy and barely able to stand before him, we are gathered up and fed with his love. The God of Jacob.

> Thank you, Lord, for loving Jacob,
> for caring for Jacob,
> for loving and caring for me.

3
The Art of Selfishness

Are you self-ish?
Are you a self-ish person?
Too self-ish?
Or not self-ish enough?
for your own good.

We do funny things with words. Like with the word, "selfish." We take an organism (self) that feels warmth and pain, that loves, feels, wants and has convictions, that can hear, see, touch, taste, and smell—and we tell it that "to be selfish is . . ." Well, "selfish" is a dirty word. And if "selfish" is a dirty word, being "un-self-ish" is clean. How carefully we condition our children! But there is a problem. And the problem for me, at least, is that I have never been precisely sure what "being un-self-ish" means. That is, unless it means being something, somebody other than me (my self).

There are a lot of ways you and I can be un-sclf-ish. We can be un-self-ish about our feelings, about our wants, and about our worlds. But things happen when are are un-self-ish. Take what happens when we are un-self-ish about our feelings. Bernard Gunther describes the process:

> LEARN TO CONFORM
> TO NOT EXPRESS:
> ACT LIKE YOUNG LADIES
> AND GENTLEMEN, BEHAVE YOURSELF
> RE-STRICT YOURSELF
> CONSTRICT YOURSELF
> YOU MUST TRY HARDER
> MAKE EFFORT
> PAY-A-TENSION.[1]

How true.

I will never forget a philosophy lecture in which the instructor was warning us against taking a point of view in philosophy. To do so, he carefully explained, would mean that we were subjective or biased—we would involve our *feelings*, which, he reminded us, "are not completely reliable." What I wanted to say to him was that I did not intend to spend the rest of my life *being completely reliable*. Life is too exciting to be completely reliable. I am too complicated to be that un-self-ish. Too much of the world wants us to be un-self-ish about our feelings.

Things happen, too, when we are un-self-ish about our wants. Most of us learned long ago that it is impolite to want. So, instead of asking, wanting or demanding anything, we wait for Santa Claus or the Good Fairy to fulfill our secret wishes.

Many psychologists comment on a curious phenomenon. Something strange happens following every Christmas. An awful lot of people enter into mild depression. It seems that nobody guessed what they *really* wanted for Christmas. They had their heart set on something special—and they didn't get it. And so, depression.

I am, I guess, a special case. For several years I received from my parents the same Christmas present: a pair of pajamas, a bathrobe, and some bedroom slippers. At one point I had the most unbelievable array of pajamas, bathrobes, and bedroom slippers imaginable. And almost all of them unused. Until I heard of Church rummage sales.

We get depressed because nobody guesses what we really want for Christmas. And the same depression and anger reappear in almost every marriage. I don't believe anything hurts more in a marriage than the hurt that accompanies the expressions: "Didn't you *know* how I felt?" "I thought you'd have *guessed. . . .*" It's as if we expected our mates to have a built-in crystal ball—one that would magically reveal our secret feelings and wants. The plain truth is that we have forgotten how to ask. So we keep getting the same old pajamas, bathrobes, and bedroom slippers. It is, after all, better to be un-self-ish.

We are un-self-ish about our feelings and our wants. And we are very un-self-ish about our worlds.

I was talking with a college student recently who said: "I spend so much of my time accommodating myself to other people's worlds that *I* seem to have gotten squeezed out, lost in the shuffle. Here I've been, all year long, waiting for *my world* to happen—and it hasn't. Maybe it is me who will have to make it happen."

She's right. Maybe it is she who will have to make it happen. It is clear that no one is standing off in the wings with a crystal ball, waiting to make things happen for her.

Think back. How many times, when you've had the impulse to do or to be something different (to disturb the dinosaurs), have you been met by what the Germans call "the ubiquitous One?" "But one never does that sort of thing." "But we just don't. . . ." "You feel guilty when. . . ." Whenever we ask who this "one" is or who this "you" is, it is always no one in particular! No one in particular.

Perhaps what we need is the wisdom of Tonto. Do you remember the time when the Lone Ranger and Tonto found themselves on the open plain surrounded by Indians? There were five hundred Indians in front of them, five hundred to their rear, and six hundred on each side. The Lone Ranger turned to Tonto with fear in his eyes and asked: "What in the world are we going to do, Tonto?" To which Tonto grinned and replied, "What do you mean, '*we*,' white man?"

We are so often so un-self-ish about our feelings, our wants and our worlds. Perhaps this is because we have been told so many times that it is not Christian to be self-ish—despite the fact that, in a profound sense, Jesus was a very self-ish person. He was not grasping, dominating, or greedy, but he, above all people, lived *his* life, danced *his* dance.

Always, they were his tears, his demands. No one ever doubted what he felt, what he wanted, what he expected. And it was very clear that it was his kind of world he was creating.

Even on the cross he was not forgetful of his self. He died largely because he refused to give away his self—his feelings toward his friends, his enemies, his Father, his wants, demands for the world, his own world. What he wanted, he wanted so much.

Jesus said, "You must be perfect." You must be perfect. What a burden! But not perfect as in:

> "Rooty, toot, toot.
> Rooty, toot, toot.
> We are the boys from the Institute.
> We don't smoke and we don't chew.
> And we don't go with the girls that do."

Or:

> LEARN TO CONFORM
> TO NOT EXPRESS
> ACT LIKE YOUNG LADIES
> AND GENTLEMEN, BEHAVE YOURSELF
> RE-STRICT YOURSELF
> CONSTRICT YOURSELF
> YOU MUST TRY HARDER
> MAKE EFFORT
> PAY-A-TENSION."[2]

"Perfect"—the Greek word means, "complete." Complete—Full —People of the Spirit. He above all persons, lived his life, danced his dance. They were his tears, his demands, and no one ever doubted what he felt, what he wanted. He was complete.

Soren Kierkegaard, speaking against what he saw as a contemptuous view of man in Christian thought, wrote: "If anyone, therefore, will not learn from Christianity to love *himself* in the right way, then neither can he love his neighbor; . . ."[3]

And that's right. But we seem willing to go to incredible lengths to *avoid* the question of self-appreciation, centering our attention rather on someone else. There is a basic craziness to all this—as in two lovers so intent on pleasing the other that each forgets how to enjoy. That's not love, it's crazy! And we, in our moral earnestness, are tempted to call it "virtue." And we, in our religiousity, are tempted to call it "Christian."

How often we use Jesus to induce guilt and self-righteous dogoodism. But churches which live by the unspoken slogan, "Salvation by Parish Activity," are hollow churches—just as people who live by the slogan, "We *must* do this for them," are hollow people. We can go through the motions. We can do our duty. We can fulfill all sorts of obligations. But that may have little to do with the kind of world into which we were reborn.

In the Bible, other words for Spirit are "Wind" and "Breath." God breathes His life into our bodies . . . completing us, fulfilling us—not re-stricting, con-stricting us. Self-ishness may be the goal and the end, because that which is most profound about us is beautiful, not ugly. "Complete."

How important it is to be in touch with the simple, basic side of my life: the world of colors and sounds and texture, the world of my wants and impulses and dreams, even the pain and loneliness and frustration of living—so long as it is *me* who is feeling.

Beneath all of this, what I am trying to say is that it is OK to be selfish. Maybe that is the only way to be in touch with the world of the Spirit. Maybe that is the only way to be in touch with what is really real, really valuable. And maybe that is the only way we can honestly love our neighbor: not from any tooth-gritting duty, not from any guilt or parental kind of "ought" or "should," but because deep down, where it's really at, at the level of the Spirit, that's me. It is OK to be you.

> "And I tell you,
> Ask, and it will be given you;
> seek, and you will find;
> knock, and it will be opened to you."

4
Prayer As Remembering

At the heart of Christian life is prayer. Yet the whole matter of prayer seems to many mystifying at best—or hopelessly confusing at worst. That is an unnecessary tragedy. It is possible to be both straightforward and helpful about prayer, though because there are so many different kinds of prayer, it is hard to know where to begin: meditation, incantation, confession, intercession, adoration, petition, exorcism: it's a big subject.

Rather than get caught up in all that, I would like to deal with something very simple—something much more basic than any specific variety of prayer. What I have in mind is a very straightforward kind of reflective prayer.

It seems to me that the hardest thing about Christian life is remembering who we are: People chosen out of the world to be God's people; people set apart from the kingdom of darkness to be light for the world; people who live by the power of the Spirit. My life begins with God and ends with God. The spirit of this community, of this nation, of this culture I live in have no power over me. As St. Paul reminds me, I am an ambassador from another power, another way of life (II Corinthians 5:19). My thought, my life, my heart are not controlled by the world—neither do they depend upon the world, for they belong to another Master.

But the temptation is to forget who we are. To be straightforward about it, the world around us can't stand who we are. It is important to the world that we see ourselves as Americans, first; that we be grateful for the middle-class way of life; grateful to technology for all the marvels of death it has produced; grateful to the American educational system, which often seems to exist primarily to feed middle-class morality and the demands of technology. The more we confuse Christian faith with the American way of life, the happier the world is. As we said, the temptation is to forget. When we act too strangely or raise too many questions about the world around us, we threaten the world. So the world makes it easy for us to forget who we are.

In James Broughton's play, *The Last Word*, Rusty Augenblick, facing the imminent destruction of the world, says to his wife in muted resignation:

> "I remember the professor told me:
> Always remember who you are.
> But now I can't remember who to remember."[1]

And now that he can't remember, his life seems to have gone out of him. It is so important to remember.

> —To remember is to have power.
>   To forget is to become at one with the world.
> —To remember is to live in the power of Resurrection.
>   To forget is to abdicate to the on-going death of the world.
> —To remember is to *know* and to *feel* that I have been chosen, set apart, empowered.

And there is a world of difference between a Christian who knows and feels he has been chosen, set apart, and empowered —and one who, though dedicated enough, forgets. One is powerful and confident. The other is, to use a biblical word, "lukewarm."

How do we remember? Perhaps better than scripture reading or study or running around doing the best of all possible good works—is with quiet time. Time alone and to yourself—five minutes, half an hour, an hour—just so long as it is quiet and uncluttered. Time set aside to reflect, in a very simple way, about three things:

> I have been chosen (by the Father);
> Set apart (in Christ);
> Empowered (through the Holy Spirit).

It is not a time for asking for anything, worrying about anything, or celebrating anything. It is just a time for getting in touch with who you really are. Remembering.

I have been chosen. I have been set apart. I am being empowered.

I have been chosen. Why? Lord knows why! I have no idea why I was chosen—*no idea*. In fact, I could give you at least forty-seven good reasons why I should *not* have been chosen. But, thank goodness, God's ways are not our ways. And perhaps the fact that God has chosen the likes of you and me to be his people means something.

"Chosen": marked with the sign of the cross and, in some powerful sense, a child of God. I know of no better illustration of the power of our "chosen-ness" than one of A. J. Langguth's marvelous fantasy lives of Jesus. He is writing about the boyhood of Jesus and this particular fantasy surely has its own reality in the Christ that is in each of us.

> Jesus opened his notebook on the study hall desk. Using the ruler from his geometry class, he drew a ledger's line down the center of one page. At the top of the left hand column he wrote "Assets" and over the other, "Liabilities." Under "Liabilities," he printed in block letters, "Impatient."
>
> Shielding the page from the girl across the aisle, he added:
> Demanding
> Self-righteous
> Proud
> Moody
> Suspicious
> Filled with doubt
> Tend toward arrogance
> With some dismay he counted the entries and began to contemplate the "Assets" column. With another look to be sure the girl couldn't see the page, he wrote, "Son of God."
> In better spirits, he closed the notebook and started on the next day's translation of Cicero.[2]

Despite all our liabilities and confusion and the dailyness of our lives, we have been chosen for eternity by a God who, for some strange reason, delights in us. Chosen.

"Set apart": in the Bible, this is one of the root meanings of the word, "holy." Holy . . . set apart . . . a sign. In the early days of Judaism certain places and things were set apart from their daily use as signs of the presence, or holiness of God. The Sabbath was a day set aside (*kodosh*) so the other six days would be seen as belonging to God. The church building is set apart as "holy space," with the intent of leading us to the fuller understanding that all space is holy (filled with the presence of God).

Jacques Ellul, the French lay theologian, in describing the way scripture defines the function of the Christian in the world, points to three key sayings of Jesus. Each involves our being set apart:

> "You are the salt of the earth."
> (put into the world as flavoring)

24

"You are the light of the world."
>(a sign of salvation)
>(light, revealing the hidden sin of the world)
"I send you forth as sheep in the midst of wolves."
>(a sign of the Lamb of God—a sacrificial community)[3]

Without salt, food is bland. Without light, the world remains in darkness. It is that kind of world.

And in our kind of world where everyone wants to be a "wolf" and few are called to play the part of "sheep," life is brutalized and crushed. Without a living witness of sacrifice, the world cannot *live* in any meaningful sense. Only sacrificial witness has the power to awaken and engage our deepest concerns.[4]

The Christian life is not a special ethic ("Do this! Don't do that!") or some special creed, but how we respond to the fact that we have been called: chosen by the Father and set apart in Christ.

And, "Empowered": again, biblically, the word the scriptures use for "spirit" is "breath;" the *pneuma,* the *ruach* of God, breathing life into our bodies, filling our lungs, making us alive—"spirited." How important it is to remember that an incredible power is surging up from the heart of the universe, sweeping through the world like the wind. The Spirit of God.

To be in touch with that power is always to have enough strength and enough courage to deal creatively with the world around us. Things may not always turn out our way—but whatever happens, we will have the power to live through it gracefully and with dignity.

One thing I firmly believe: The universe is teeming with the power of God—and we only shortchange ourselves when we forget that, and look instead to the applause and approval of the world for our strength.

"Empowered": I think Eastern religions are on to something when they link prayer to the simple art of breathing: sitting in front of a candle, breathing in the light . . . exhaling our own darkness. Putting it another way, filling our lungs with the *ruach,* the Spirit of God . . . exhaling our own emptiness. Breathing, the cosmic rhythm. It may be as simple as that.

We have been chosen—set apart—empowered. The first task of prayer is to remember this. And, it seems to me, the closer I am to these things, the easier everything else falls into place—whether it is adoration, thanksgiving, confessing my sin, asking for myself and others, or just getting through another day. We speak so disparagingly about looking out on the world through rose colored glasses; perhaps the image ought to be "spirit spectacles." To look out on the world through spirit spectacles is to live out our lives with the constant awareness that the world is filled with the presence and the power of Spirit.

Remembering: that's the key—and, I think, the priority of prayer. As an indication of just how important remembering is, consider the story of IALAC, which has been sweeping the nation's college campuses. IALAC stands for "I Am Lovable And Capable."

Most of us—either when we wake up in the morning or shortly after our second cup of coffee—feel pretty good. We look forward to most of what the day holds and have a strong feeling that we are both lovable and capable. It's nice to be alive. If you were to make the effort, you could easily picture yourself wearing a namecard on your chest with "I Am Lovable And Capable" written across it.

Showered and dressed and with our IALAC sign in place we are prepared to deal with the world. But then the world goes to work. At the breakfast table comes the first sally: "Are we out of eggs *again*? Why on earth didn't you buy some at the store yesterday?" And we feel a small piece of our "I Am Lovable And Capable" sign being torn off at the corner.

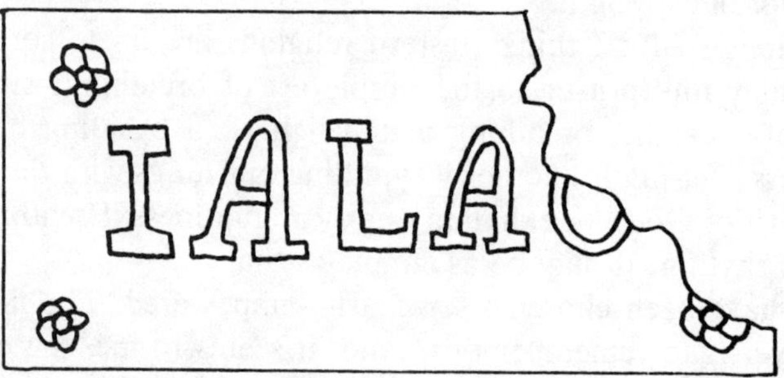

But you recover nicely and enjoy a leisurely ride to an appointment in the city, enjoying the freshness of the day, especially alive to the world around you. But your casual pace has made you late, and despite gracious apologies, you are greeted with a glare and slightly clenched teeth. Off comes another corner of your IALAC sign.

Leaving your appointment you are met by an old friend who greets you with, "Say, are you gaining weight—or is it that suit you're wearing?" Another part of your sign is in tatters.

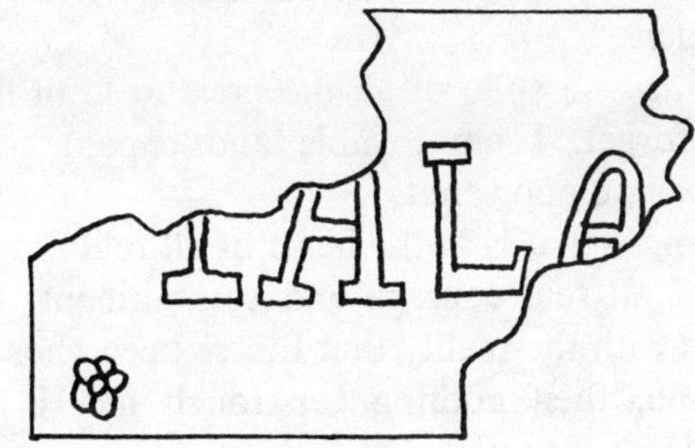

Having lunch with other friends, you attempt to be helpful in what for them is a very difficult situation—but you get nowhere. There was nothing you could do. And so goes yet another part of what began as a lovely sign.

Finally back home your next door neighbor calls, "I just wanted to thank you for your help with our plants. It made all the difference." Great! You paste part of your sign back together. But somehow it's not the same.

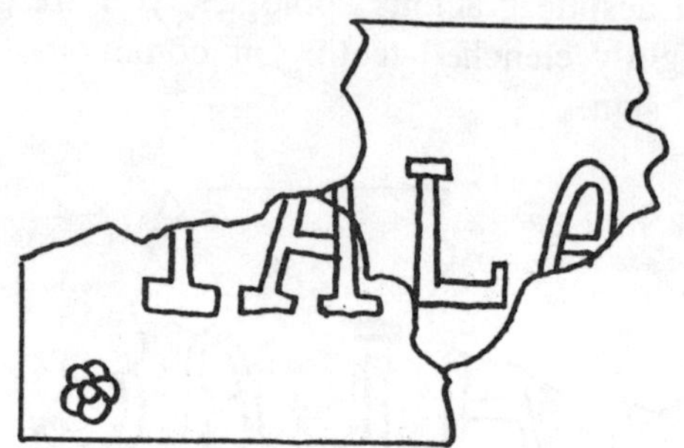

It doesn't take too much of the day before our IALAC sign is in shreds. It's a wonder that we have left any sense whatsoever that we are in any way lovable and capable. I listen to myself as I deal with my own children: "Come on, let's eat!" "Hey! You're getting cereal all over the floor!" "Hurry up, you're going to make us all late!" "That's enough noise!"

How they survive all that with humor and self-love is a miracle of the first order.

Remembering—in spite of all the pressures, all the incredible pressures to forget. I am lovable and capable. I have been chosen, set apart, empowered.

Remembering—that is at the heart of all real prayer. And it is at the heart of all real courage and commitment. If I am even dimly in touch with the reality that I have been chosen, set apart, and empowered, then nothing can touch me. I have already passed from death into life.

Whether it is five minutes of quiet time at the beginning or middle of the day—or sitting quietly before a candle, inhaling the light and power of the Holy Spirit—the point is to remember.

5

The Church (I):
The Hands of God

A few evenings ago my five-year-old daughter was finishing up what, for her, had been a disastrous day. Everything had gone wrong. She had received rough treatment at the hands of her friends, near incessant criticism from her parents, and the usual quota of trouble from her older brother. The morning's joyful enthusiasm had been given over to evening resignation and depression.

But, mercifully, bedtime had come. As I went into Jennifer's room for prayers, she looked up at me with doleful eyes and asked quietly, "Daddy, could we sing the song about the hands?"

That, for me, was an incredibly moving moment. Out of all her disappointment and hurt, she had reached out for one of the most powerful of all religious images:

> "He's got the whole world in his hands.
> He's got the whole wide world in his hands.
> He's got the whole world in his hands,
> He's got the whole world in his hands.
>
> "He's got Jennifer Woodward in his hands.
> He's got Jennifer Woodward in his hands.
> He's got Jennifer Woodward in his hands.
> He's got the whole world in his hands."

He's got the whole world in his hands: a powerful image. He holds us, He sustains us, He keeps us in life; in his hands. A powerful image. In fact, an image so overwhelming that a popular TV commercial has used it to push insurance. The allusion is so simple, or so outrageous that it would be a crime not to follow it through—or to turn it upside down.

"He's got the Whole World In His Hands." There are those special moments when I really feel in his hands. Sometimes there is a pat on the back to encourage me, an arm around my shoulder to console me, or a slap on my fanny to correct me. And there are those times, for all of us, when, in desperation, we want only to throw ourselves into the loving hands of God.

"Into your hands, Father, I commend my Spirit."

Saint Paul writes of the hands of the potter; creating us, molding us, giving shape and beauty to our lives. Jeremiah, the prophet, speaks (almost) of the hands of God *shoving* him out into the world to speak the truth he knows in his heart, but is afraid to speak with his lips. The Psalmist, in moments of quiet passion, speaks of the hands of God enfolding us.

I

The Hands of God.
"He's got the whole world in his hands,"
molding us, comforting us,
sending us out.

This is all well and good;
but part of the Biblical witness is that God,
in effect, has turned the tables on us.
He has put himself in our hands.

A basic truth about Jesus Christ;
He was not some celestial ruler,
carefully keeping the appropriate divine distance from
    scruffy mortals.
Not at all.
The Father, quite literally, put him into our hands:

His mother held him to her breast and nursed him,
Small children touched him,
Sick people tugged at his sleeves,
Soldiers slapped his face
and Thomas examined his wounds.

The life of God was put into our hands.

The immense and cosmic deity, all of a sudden was
    very small and very fragile . . .
entrusted to the likes of you and me.

There is a great temptation to believe otherwise: to think of God as the untouchable, unreachable sovereign of the universe.

A young man, in considerable anguish, went to see his pastor for counselling. After the young man had laid out his very difficult and sensitive situation, the pastor leaned back in his chair, folded his hands, and said in a soft, soothing manner, "Well, when I find myself confused about what to do, I always ask myself what Jesus would have done in my situation."
"I know that, Pastor," the young man replied, "but I really don't think Jesus would ever have gotten himself involved in the kind of mess I'm in!"

How difficult it is to be comfortable about the human reality of Jesus. And how tempting it is to believe that Jesus was "different," that he wasn't really like us—especially sexually.

A friend of mine, in a Sunday School setting, was in great distress. After sustaining a barrage of youthful questions on the order of, "Did Jesus ever go to the bathroom?" he was finally driven to the point of sheer desperation.

The only way out was to strike back with his own naive question: "All right! If Jesus were taking a bath, would there be any difference between *him* taking a bath and one of *you* taking a bath?"

One child yelled out, "Of course."

My friend, intrigued at a possible difference, asked, "OK. What's the difference?"

"That's easy," the child said. "Jesus wouldn't leave a ring around the tub."

How *enormous* we make God out to be! How *unreachable,* how *untouchable* we make him; despite the fact that he has made himself small, touchable. He put himself into our hands.

II

One of the ways God communicates his power to us is through Bread and Wine. Food put into our hands. The symbol of food is appropriate because as food is assimilated, it loses its own nature and takes on ours. And this is how it is with the life of Christ: it shapes itself in our own life and action. Men and women fed with the life of Christ are always more fully themselves for the gift.
A funny thing about God: He doesn't try to shape us into

pre-cut molds like Harold Holy or Susan Sanctity. Instead, he shapes *himself* into real people: you and me. He always seems to become most real in people and in communities.

III

> He has put himself in our hands:
> in the person of Jesus,
> in the symbols, gifts of his power
> and then, quite literally,
> his life is in our hands.
>
> My hands—your hands—
> whether they are baby soft,
> arthritic,
> or dishpan red;
> they are the hands of God in the world.
> He has no other hands or feet or eyes in the world.
> We're it.
> What we touch and how we touch are all important.
>
> The Body of Christ.
> For St. Paul (who coined the phrase)
> this is no simple metaphor,
> but a powerful statement about the way things are.
>
> The Body of Christ.
> The life of God made small,
> real,
> believable—
> in a community of persons.

$$6$$

The Church (II):
The People of God

Many people are disillusioned about the Church. I think part of that disillusionment stems from the tendency of church people (including, of course, myself) to "play" at Christianity, making it trivial. To give you an example: it is very easy to "play" at Resurrection. "Christ is risen!" That's fine. That's happy news. But I am not always too sure what that says about how I will live my life. Because the Resurrection that is really important was either *back then*, as a special sign or symbol. Or it's coming . . . as the main feature, which follows whatever it is we're involved in now (the cartoon, the travelogue, or the documentary, according to one's special circumstances). So Resurrection has become for us an exciting relic—either past or future.

That is a cop out. It is, of course, nothing less than a convenient way of refusing to deal with the reality of who we are as a people:

> "You are a chosen race, a royal priesthood, a holy nation, God's own people."
>
> I PETER 2:9

Now that is a powerful statement about who we are. And it is a difficult statement to take seriously, because it asks us to minimize that thing we hold so precious: our guilt. Despite the noble truth that God is far less interested in our guilt than in our liberation, most of us treat the New Testament pretty much as if it were an essay in guilt. I remember the way it was once presented to me:

> St. Paul and all the rest will tell you how to be a "good boy"
> Meaning: a controlled boy,
> > an obedient boy,
> > unaware of the surge of life and power
> > coursing through my body.
> "We are good people: we are Christians."

How tame. How conventional. How demoralizing.

But the word is that we have died to all that. Proving our manhood, proving our femininity, proving that we are OK as children of God—we have died to all that. That is the point. That war is over (despite the fact that many of us are like the Japanese soldier who stayed in hiding for nearly 30 years because he thought World War II was still going on).

"You are a chosen race . . . "
That's right: chosen.
Maybe for all the wrong reasons;
maybe for some of the right reasons.
But chosen: that's the inescapable part.

You are a chosen race:
you don't have to spend the rest of your life
proving you "should have been chosen."
That is the cop out.

"A holy nation."
A people set apart.
That is what "holy" means: "set apart."
Not just "commanded to love,"
but freed to love—
because we have been set within a community
where it is OK to love,
to "con-celebrate"
as brothers and sisters of a new world.

New World
(that's important);
not the old world (as much as we want to live there);
    "Don't expect much, Lord,
    I'm only human."

That's the cop out.

"A royal priesthood."
not wearing fancy clothes,
but as free men and women,
standing in the middle
of the incredible mess the world has made of itself,
and offering it all up

    feeling its pain,

     in touch with its horror,
     celebrating its victories,

and raising it all up.

A chosen race
A holy nation
Royal Priesthood.

You can't hack it if you haven't been chosen.
We can't make it if we're not a nation.
We can't offer it up if we haven't,
in some mysterious way,
been set apart.

God's own people.

     With salvation,
     in its most important sense,
     behind us.

       With resurrection,
       in its most important sense,
       upon us.

Alleluia! We are risen.
We are risen, indeed. Alleluia!

Anything less is a cop out.

7
The Church (III): Irrelevance, Its Task

For fear of offending someone, I'll apologize in advance. I'm sorry. But this is a touchy subject: our task, as the Church, is to be irrelevant to the world around us. You have read it correctly: irrelevant.

Irrelevant: our task, as the Church, if you've read or seen "Zorba the Greek," is to be something like Zorba. If you saw the movie, "Alice's Restaurant," something like Arlo Guthrie's careless, innocent, almost divine-mystical kind of irrelevance, where producing, measuring up, being a "good person" (whatever that means), simply have no meaning.

If you and I are being relevant, we ask: "How can I be a better person? A more productive person?" If we are being irrelevant, we ask: "How can I be a more joyous, spontaneous, alive, aware person?"

"Relevant Christianity" usually involves pretty heavy, serious stuff: doing good works and carrying enormous responsibilities. And almost everywhere you find "relevant Christianity," you find all the "relevant questions" being asked: "Why aren't we more loving? Why aren't we doing more? Why aren't we giving more? Helping more?" If you listen carefully, you can pick up the litany: "Not enough! Not enough! Not enough!" And the beat goes on. "Not enough." Or in the words of the un-song, "What the world needs now is guilt, sweet guilt."

Well, no. That's overstating it . . . isn't it? But if so, why is it that the best loved sermons always seem to be those that give us hell?

> "How was the minister this morning?"
> "Fantastic! He really gave it to us this morning."

How relevant!

So, on Sunday mornings, crazy people that they are, Christians go to a banquet. That's one of the names for Holy Communion:

"banquet." Despite the fact that we are hung up, hung down, dragged in, dragged out, and there is so much to do, so very much to do, so very much more to do—God says, "*Join the banquet!*"

And so, Eucharist: singing songs, praising God, sharing Bread and Wine, and just being together as the people of God. And there needn't be any ulterior motive—just doing it is enough. How marvellously irrelevant!

So what's the big deal about being irrelevant? Rabbi Abraham Heschel said it:

> God has ordered this world so that every little girl will be a princess and every little boy a prince.

It seems to me that we, despite all the evidence to the contrary, must continue to say just that—that a human being is not a number, that he or she should not be folded, stamped, spindled, or mutilated. In the words of Rowland Cox:

> Man is not primarily a performer of tasks, but one who weeps and laughs and hopes and prays in an incredibly varied world where nothing is just what it seems, that he was made for eternity and what's more, he is going to make it to eternity.[1]

And maybe (just maybe) the only way men and women are going to *understand* this is through a Christianity which shows the presence of a totally other dimension than the pragmatic, the functional—the relevant. Words are not adequate to this task. Symbols may be:

> The clown in the midst of an up-tight world.
> The ballerina in the Oval Office.
> The small child wandering through the Board of Directors meeting.
> The priest dressed in long, flowing, brightly colored robes in the middle of a prayer meeting.

Several people have remarked that perhaps the one adequate symbol of Christ in our modern world is the clown—a fool wandering through life accepting its pain but living a dimension of life that calls us out of our self-made complications into divine simplicity. Buster Keaton may have more to say about divine reality than Billy Graham.

Touching on this same reality is the hymn by Sidney Carter, "The Lord of the Dance."

I danced in the morning when the world was begun
And I danced in the moon and stars and the sun,
And I came down from heaven and I danced on the earth,
At Bethlehem I had my birth.

> CHORUS:
> *Dance, then, wherever you may be,*
> *I am the Lord of the Dance, said he,*
> *And I'll lead you all, wherever you may be,*
> *and I'll lead you all in the Dance, said he.*

I danced for the scribe and the pharisee,
They would not come and they would not follow me.
I danced for the fishermen, for James and John,
They came with me and the dance goes on.

> (chorus:)

I danced on the Sabbath and I cured the lame,
The holy people said it was a shame.
They whipped and they stripped me and they hung me high
And left me there on a cross to die.

I danced on a Friday when the sky turned black,
It's hard to dance with the devil on your back.
They buried my body and they thought I'd gone,
But I am the dance and I still go on.

> (chorus:)

They cut me down and I leapt up high—
I am the life that will never, never die.
I'll live in you if you live in me—
I am the Lord of the lance said he[2]

How foreign this is to the grim determination with which we attempt to manipulate both ourselves and the world around us. How easy it is to miss the point of life by our constant attention to the practical, the pragmatic, the relevant.

Even religion, itself, has come to be something to make work, to believe—not to be danced. And the results have been disastrous. Witness the protest by a young college student:

"I refuse to be put into any kind of religious straight-jacket. I believe in grace, but when I look around me in church, everyone seems so rigid, so grim. I value my freedom too much to get caught up in that!"

If the medium is the message, the message is hardly gospel ("good news").

Perhaps every seminary curriculum should include the art of juggling—and Confirmation classes a healthy bit of play and dance.

So what is the big deal about being irrelevant? Perhaps a couple of examples would be helpful.

The Christian faith tries to say that sex is not just a function. It is not just for making babies, or relieving tension. It is also fun, joyous. And it is to be enjoyed, celebrated—as in "banquet."

How easy that is to say—but ask almost anyone who does marriage counselling, and he or she will tell you how *remote* we are from this understanding. How locked in we are to "Relevant Sex"—measuring up, producing good feelings, performing.

> "Am I OK?"
> "Was I really good?"
> "I didn't do anything wrong, did I?"

I remember the Locker Room Criteria of high school days. And despite the *Playboy* Philosophy and cries of a sexual revolution, it hasn't really changed:

> "Did you turn her on?"
> "Oh, man, I really snowed her!"

Not, "Were you free to be yourself with her? . . . And enjoy yourself in the relationship? . . . With or without sex?" But:

> "How did you function?"

The awful end-product of all this is a man and woman living together, each so hell-bent on functioning well, on pleasing the other, that each (in his or her own way) forgets to enjoy, to celebrate, to banquet. Both are being *too relevant* to one another! How easy it is to miss the point of life.

To be sure, Irrelevant, Banquet sex does not mean irresponsible sex, which, despite the advertisements, is rarely very joyous. It is hardly an occasion for celebration—and usually a pretty sour banquet.

How easy it is to miss the point—by being so persistently relevant.

And education. It seems to me that despite our attempts to make it a kind of down payment for getting ahead, we of the Christian faith have got to demand that it, too, must have its own irrelevance. I think it was Paul Goodman who said, "Giving an acceptable interpretation of 'Ode to a Grecian Urn' somehow means you will live in a better suburb . . . and drive a bigger car." If you don't believe that, count the times you have heard, or said, "As soon as you are finished with your homework, you can go out and play." As if discovery weren't one of the highest forms of play!

How demeaning to the Father who created all things, and who chose through Jesus to identify himself totally with this very thingy universe—to sell education, learning, discovery on the basis that a college degree will earn you more money. Blasphemy often comes in respectable wrappers.

It seems to me that there is something religious, *deeply* religious, in the joy of discovery—in playing around, battling with ideas and things—even though the whole enterprise may be totally irrelevant to the functional, pragmatic world we live in.

So what does it mean, that our task is to be irrelevant? That my pain, my conflicts, my commitments, or work in the world are unimportant? No. But it does mean that they are only half the story.

> I danced on the Sabbath and I cured the lame,
> The holy people said it was a shame.
> They whipped and they stripped me and they hung me high.
> And left me there on a cross to die.

The other side of the story is that I am loved and cared for in ways I can't even conceive. And despite all the things in me that say otherwise, I have been chosen for eternity and given the name, "A Child of God." In spite of the conventional wisdom of the world, there is the Banquet side of life.

> *Dance, then, wherever you may be,*
> *I am the Lord of the Dance, said he,*
> *And I'll lead you all, wherever you may be,*
> *And I'll lead you all in the Dance, said he.*

Christian Ethics: A Matter of Vision—Not Violation

"Do you know what a word is?" the poet whispered in the middle of a long and technical discussion. I hemmed and hawed and stuttered and mumbled (afraid of saying either "Yes" or "No") for some time. My friend, the poet, then ended my discomfort by shouting, *"It's a four letter word!"*

As a fellow purveyor of words, I laughed. Words can take on a life of their own (as in a book). They can stand between experience and people (as in Jules Feiffer's wonderful cartoon sequence of an old man sitting in a rocking chair):

> "I used to think I was poor.
> "Then they told me I wasn't poor. I was 'needy.'
> "Then they told me it was self-defeating to think of
>   myself as needy, I was 'deprived.'
> "Then they told me deprived was a bad image,
>   I was 'underprivileged.'
> "Then they told me underprivileged was overused,
>   I was 'disadvantaged.'
> "I still don't have a dime.
> "But I have a great vocabulary."

How many times have I heard a radio evangelist go on and on, attempting to manipulate his listeners into accepting a certain definition of "righteousness"—only to switch my radio with the retort. "What possible difference does *that* make?"

It's obvious; saying something is true doesn't make it true, just as saying something is right, moral, or ethical does not make it so. This is the problem with "Christian ethics." "Rule," like "word," is a four letter word—no matter how classed up it may be with holy adjectives.

A short while ago I was with a group of people trying to come up with an adequate meaning for the word, "commitment." People had made several valiant, but unhelpful suggestions.

Many words had been offered to explain the one word. Then one person said, "When I think of commitment, I remember the fellow who used to live next door to us."

"One summer evening I saw him out in his backyard walking back and forth across a long 2x4 board. This went on for a couple of evenings until I saw him stringing a heavy clothesline about two feet off the ground between two poles.

"For the next three weeks he was out there every evening, walking back and forth, gaining confidence and agility.

"Then one evening he had stretched a thin cable about fifteen feet in the air. He was walking back and forth along it. First with a balancing pole, then after a few more weeks, with only his sense of balance to keep him from falling.

"When it got to be late autumn, he had become a master of the high wire. Once on the wire he would jump up and down, do cartwheels and juggle—surviving heavy winds, rainstorms, and bitter cold. Well before this time I had begun a nightly ritual of watching him from the comfort of my own breakfast room. But we had never spoken.

"Then one night I saw him up on the wire pushing a wheelbarrow back and forth, back and forth—sometimes running with it, other times walking behind it blindfolded. I could contain myself no longer. I left my house and went up to him and said, 'I don't know if you have noticed me watching you from my window, but I want to say how much I've enjoyed watching you work. I think you are incredible! I don't think there is anything you couldn't do on that high wire . . . you are magnificent!'

"He mumbled his thanks.

" 'But there is one thing I don't understand. It's that wheelbarrow. Do you mind my asking what all this means?

" 'Of course not,' he said. 'Next month I am going to wheel someone in this wheelbarrow across the Grand Canyon on a high wire.'

" 'Fantastic!' I said. 'I want you to know that I have absolute faith in you. You can do it. If anyone has ever had confidence in another person, I've got confidence in you. I'd be willing to bet any amount of money you'll make it.'

" 'That's good to hear,' he said, 'because I've been looking for someone to ride in the wheelbarrow.' "

A story. It took a story to settle the issue. And once the story had been told, there was no more need for words and definitions.

Despite the variations in ritual, symbols, and official creeds, there are basically two kinds of religion. There is the religion of the sign:

ONE WAY. "No, No." "Do this! Don't do that!"
And there is the religion of the story:

> There was a man who had two sons; and the younger of them
> said to his father, "Father, give me the share of the property
> which belongs to me."

The best thing about religion of the sign is that it tells us pretty much what is expected of us. On the positive side, the sign tells us the basic ingredients of being a good person, a holy person, a person acceptable to God (even the most lofty theologies of grace usually, when under pressure, give us some indications of what it means—behaviorally—to accept God's free gift of love and acceptance).

The religion of the sign also tells us what will get us in trouble —in trouble with ourselves, our fellow human beings, and with God.

> "Thou shalt have none other gods but me," unless you want to
> be shortchanged, to stand on the sidelines of human life.

> "Thou shalt not steal," unless you wish to destroy the order of
> love built into the universe—and destroy yourself and others in
> the process.

Most of us, for better or worse, grew up nurtured by a steady diet of religion of the sign.

At its best, religion of the sign has all the attractiveness of a warm, loving parent guiding a child into maturity, introducing the child to the beauty of fulfilling relationships, warning and admonishing the child about destructive relationships and behavior.

The authentic core of the Jewish Law (the most complete expression of the religion of the sign) was not meant to be restrictive or deadening. It was a gift from God and was intended to be liberating. Frederick Buechner, perhaps, says it best in his marvellous little book, *Wishful Thinking: A Theological ABC*:

> LAW
>
> There are basically two kinds: (1) law as the way things
> ought to be, and (2) law as the way things are. An example of
> the first is NO TRESPASSING. An example of the second is the
> law of gravity.
>
> God's Law has traditionally been spelled out in terms of cate-
> gory No. 1, a compendium of do's and don'ts. These do's and

don'ts are the work of moralists and when obeyed serve the useful purpose of keeping us from each other's throats. They can't make us human but they can keep us honest.

God's Law *in itself*, however, comes under category No. 2 and is the work of God. It has been stated in eight words: "He who does not love remains in death." (I John 3:14) Like it or not, that's how it is. If you don't believe it, you can always put it to the test just the way if you don't believe the law of gravity, you can always step out a tenth-story window.[1]

That is the religion of the sign at its best. At its worst it is more like a drill sergeant than a loving parent:

> "Don't touch that part of his/her body until you are married!"

> "Real Christians do not experiment with marijuana."

> "In your vocation you will be productive for the common good."

> "It is incumbent upon every Christian to give ten percent of current income to the Church for the furtherance of God's work in the world."

Some of this may be very helpful to some people—especially nervous and insecure people. But while it may keep them (us) in line, it really has very little to do with what life is really about. In real life situations, it is not of much use. Consider this: Most of us would give a four-year-old boy a toy gun. Few of us would give a fourteen-year-old boy a copy of *Playboy*. Which of the two —toy gun or *Playboy* magazine—is the more obscene?

To be sure, "He who does not love remains in death." So far, so good. But when we move beyond the general (vague) terms and begin to speak about specifics, all hell breaks loose:

> How do I love my neighbor who daily barrages me with unmitigated neurotic whining? Hang in there with him—comforting and supporting him? Or do I proceed to obtain a court order, committing him to psychiatric care?

> How could we have best loved the South Vietnamese—by killing and being killed for them (if so, we have loved and still remain in death)? Or should we have left them to their own fate, however dubious and self-destructive that might have been?[2]

It's a complicated business. And in the final analysis, "love" may be just another four letter word.

The sign promises security. All well and good. But the sign, it seems to me, can never really deliver on its promise. No matter how high the rules are piled, no matter how tightly woven the security blanket, there remains something elusive, something very human that the rules and the signs cannot encompass.[3]

The difference between the religion of the sign and the religion of the story is all the difference between a living, dynamic faith and a dead(ly) creed. Take the whole matter of money: How much should I give to charities, charity, to the United Fund, the Church? What's left over after the bills are paid? A tithe? A "modern" tithe (5%) or the Biblical tithe (10%)? If I tithe, do I base it on gross income or adjusted gross income? What agony! It pains me to admit that I have sat through several "helpful" sermons about this very thing without once coughing, yawning, or causing at least a minor diversion. I suppose my reasons for not doing so were a mixture of courtesy and wanting, myself, "to do what's right." But what incredible agony!

> The rabbi of Sasov once gave the last money he had in his pocket to a notoriously disreputable man.
>
> The rabbi's disciples were both shocked and disappointed. They began to scold their master. But when they had had their say, Sasov answered them: "Shall I be more finicky than God, who gave it to me?"

A story. And, I think, a disturbing story. Something inside me is enormously moved by that rabbi's simple sense of dependence upon God. And at the same time something else inside me is fighting the story, wanting to analyze away the claims it makes upon me. But whatever the outcome inside me, I *am* involved. The story leaves me free to be captured by its gentle vision—and free to rationalize it all away as absurd. But, through the story, I am "hooked."

The really remarkable thing about this particular story is its similarity in force to the Sermon on the Mount. The pronouncements of Jesus in the Sermon on the Mount ("You have heard that it was said . . . but I say to you") have the same double qualities of persuasiveness and absurdity as the simple tale of the rabbi of Sasov.

> "You have heard that it was said, 'You shall not commit adultery.' But I say to you that every one who looks at a woman lustfully has already committed adultery with her in his heart. If your right eye causes you to sin, pluck it out and throw it away; it is better that you lose one of your members than that your whole body be thrown into hell. And if your right hand causes

you to sin, cut it off and throw it away; it is better that you lose one of your members than that your whole body go into hell."

MATTHEW 5:27–30

"You have heard that it was said, 'An eye for an eye and a tooth for a tooth.' But I say to you, Do not resist one who is evil. But if any one strikes you on the right cheek, turn to him the other also; and if any one would sue you and take your coat, let him have your cloak as well; and if any one forces you to go one mile, go with him two miles. Give to him who begs from you, and do not refuse him who would borrow from you."

MATTHEW 5:38–42

While these *look* like commandments (signs) and *sound* like commandments—something else is going on. Certainly as "guides for successful living" they just don't stand up! And as signposts for a moral life they seem way beyond my own humble reach. So how are we to treat them?

Dietrich Bonhoeffer, wrestling with this very question, wrote:

> If we decided not to take it literally, we should be evading the seriousness of the commandment, and if, on the other hand, we decided it was to be taken literally, we should at once reveal the absurdity of the Christian position, and thereby invalidate the commandment. The fact that we receive no answer to the question only makes the commandment even more inescapable.[4]

There it is again, the double quality of persuasiveness and absurdity. How similar are the bits and pieces of the Sermon on the Mount to short, pointed stories. Each, in its own setting, surprises and enlightens. Each captures and involves its hearers. And each is open-ended, calling for personal response—the sort which depends in some important way on the particular person responding. Each with the double quality of persuasiveness and absurdity.

One of the key moral issues of this decade is the environmental issue. What about our response to the world around us? The specifics are innumerable: thermostat control, off-shore drilling, strip mining, littering, endangered species, and the needs of economic growth. But what, one asks, is the proper *religious* response? But to ask the question (if we are only asking for signs and rules) may only be to avoid the issue. There may be a better way:

> Once two people came before Rabbi Ezekiel Landau, each claiming ownership of a certain tract of land. After listening to

their arguments, Ezekiel Landau said, "Take me to the land."

The two men took the rabbi to the piece of land in dispute. Once there Ezekiel Landau said, "Let the earth itself render judgment." And to the utter amazement of the two men, he placed his ear to the ground and listened.

After a few moments he stood up. He turned to the two men and announced, "The earth has rendered its decision: 'I belong to neither of you, but both of you belong to me.' "

Again a story. A simple, delightful absurd story. But a story which points beyond all signs (the disputants were looking for signs) to a very special vision of how things are.

A vision. That, of course, is the key. And when we set about to share our visions with one another, stories (and pictures) always turn out to be the best means we have for doing so. So it is no coincidence that the way of Jesus, with almost no exceptions, was not through signs, but stories:[5]

A sower went out to sow. . . .
There was a man who gave a great banquet. . . .
There was a rich man who dressed in purple and fine linen.
What shall I compare the Kingdom of God to?

Religion of the story is, at its heart, religion of the vision. And it is here that we begin to understand Christian ethics in its deepest and most beautiful form.

Deepest—because it is, I believe, only through the story and the picture that I am grasped most completely. I can obey and give allegiance to rules and signs, but only the story can touch me where I live; only the story can hope to call forth what is most profound about me.

Most beautiful—because an open response to the Christian vision is beautiful in much the same way the child's response to the vision of fairy tales is beautiful. And beautiful because whenever gentle persuasiveness and the absurd are joined (as in children's play, the circus clown, and Mozart), we have all the potential for a special kind of loveliness and beauty.

Christian ethics is not a new and better set of proscriptions and admonitions, do's and don'ts, rules and regulations. Despite the form, that is certainly not what lies behind even the Sermon on the Mount. Even there, what we begin to sense, beyond the Law, is a very special and radical vision of how human beings are to be related to one another and to the One who is above (beneath) all things.

There is a beautiful word in the New Testament for sin. The

word is "*hamartia*." The root of the word is "missing the mark," as in archery. It is not violation of this, that, or the other rule—but missing the bull's-eye, getting shortchanged (or shortchanging ourselves). Missing the mark has to do with vision, not violation. Whereas the Law was given for "the hardness of our hearts" (Mark 10:5–9), the vision is given to entice us, to capture us, to woo us.

The distinction between vision and violation is an important one. Over and over again, we see it worked out in Jesus' own life and ministry:

> And he went on from there, and entered their synagogue. And behold, there was a man with a withered hand. And they asked him, "Is it lawful to heal on the sabbath?" so that they might accuse him. He said to them, "What man of you, if he has one sheep and it falls into a pit on the sabbath, will not lay hold of it and lift it out? Of how much more value is a man than a sheep! So it is lawful to do good on the sabbath." Then he said to the man, "Stretch out your hand." And the man stretched it out, and it was restored, whole like the other. But the Pharisees went out and took counsel against him, how to destroy him.
>
> MATTHEW 12:9–14

The Law was very clear: no work, no healing on the Sabbath (except in the case of imminent death). And it was also clear that to break one of the laws was to have violated them all. It may be hard for us to understand the force of this scene. Try to imagine the outrage Americans might feel at a citizens' group kidnapping all the members of the oil lobby in Washington. D.C. on the eve of an important vote on off-shore drilling, and saying at a press conference, "The legislative process was created to serve the people, and not the oil interests." If you can grasp that, you are probably close to the feeling. There are laws, after all. And if people go about doing what *they* think is right in spite of the rules, everything is threatened. We are, as we say, "a nation of laws, not of men." Get it? The Pharisees did.

But the problem for twentieth-century America, as well as for first-century Jesus, is that law may stand in the way of hitting the mark. So, like it or not, Jesus was not very good about following rules.

It was not that he was lacking clear directions, a clear understanding of the Law, or a group of people around him to point out his obvious duty in an given situation; almost daily he was surrounded by people who told him what to do, what his obligations were, how to live his life:

The Pharisees carefully explained the Law to him.

Peter, like a wise father, told him that he was only buying trouble, doing the things he was doing.

Mary, like a wise mother, told him to go slowly, "Don't make a fool of yourself. . . ."

Judas, like a first-century Jerry Rubin, urged him to go faster, "You're not making enough trouble, enough waves."

But Jesus, in all he did, seemed to ignore them all. And he seemed to ignore them all with a special kind of freedom. He didn't threaten anyone: "If you don't let me do it my way, you'll be sorry." And he wasn't really a rebel, like the person who says with clenched teeth: "I don't care *who* says it's right, or how many people say its right. Nobody is going to tell *me* how to vote, how to act, how to behave!"

Jesus responded not by threat or rebellion, but with freedom and integrity. The difference between Jesus and the people who surrounded him was that Jesus lived not by the sign but by a vision. It was a special vision of what it means to be a human being, with other human beings, as children of the one Father.

Not by law (security) but by a vision—and nothing less than human was to stand in the way of that vision. No one could tell him how to live his life, because he was on to something altogether new and different.

How different Jesus is from our own way of rationalization and petty rebellion. "That's OK for you, but I'm different! I'm a special case." Or the breathless words spoken from countless automobile back seats and motel rooms, "I know it's wrong, but this is different." And how different Jesus is from our own kinds of authoritarianism: "Just do as I do, and you'll get along. I'll guarantee your security."

So who is going to tell us how to live our lives? Guarantee our moral security? Jesus lived not by law but by a vision. The only "How To" that I can remember Jesus giving was to the rich young ruler (Luke 18:18–23). "Sell what you have (law) . . . and follow me" (the vision). The sign may be important, but only as prelude to the vision.

What does it mean to live by the vision? The old sermon illustration has it this way:

Once a man approached three bricklayers. And he asked each the same question: "What are you doing?" The first said,

"Making a buck." The second answered, "Laying a brick." And the third replied, "I'm building a cathedral."

"I'm building a cathedral." That, I think, is what Saint Paul is talking about when he says, "I beseech you to walk worthy of the vocation wherewith you are called. . . ." (Ephesians 4:1) The vocation—always beyond the buck, always beyond laying a brick, raising a child, selling a product, writing a book.

Building a cathedral. That's what it's all about. That is gospel, good news. It is not having a preacher, teacher, or mini-God (whatever the form it takes) telling you what to do every minute of your life. But a whole, different thing altogether. Cathedral building.

In this day and age the Christian faith is having a hard time, if we can so interpret its failure to make a decisive difference in people's lives. The problem, in part, is that we Christians are seeking adherents rather than fellow pilgrims. Adherents expect, and many find, something definite, something permanent, something unchanging upon which to depend. In the language of Wall Street, they are looking for blue chip religion. Somehow our fear, our frustrations and insecurities work against us, compressing the vision to the sign, to the durable and helpful. But while the Christian faith is definitely "high quality," it is certainly not made of the durability and cautious optimism of the blue chip. It is much, much more risky and adventuresome.

In religion, as with so many other things, we need to be reminded, in Sheldon Kopp's metaphor, that the cool water of the running stream may be scooped up with open, overflowing palms. It cannot be *grasped* up to the mouth with clenching fists, no matter what thirst motivates our desperate grab.[6]

It is easy to stick with the stodgy line, settling for blue chips and AAA bonds. It is difficult to re-learn the fine art of religion of the story, quieting for a moment our demands for the specific, the particular, the practical. We can see our predicament in the old Zen story of the three young pupils whose master instructs them that they must spend a time in complete silence if they are to be enlightened:

"Remember, not a word from any of you," he admonishes. Immediately, the first pupil says, "I shall not speak at all." "How stupid you are: why did you talk?" says the second. "I am the only one who has not spoken," concludes the third.[7]

A final word (and then a gift): For some reason it is easier to teach by rules and signs. That is the awful temptation confronting all teachers and preachers. If you want something more, you may have to ask for it. There is usually some reason why pearls of great price are so darned expensive.

THE GIFT*

When the great Rabbi Israel Baal Shem-Tov saw misfortune threatening the Jews it was his custom to go into a certain part of the forest to meditate. There he would light a fire, say a special prayer, and the miracle would be accomplished and the misfortune averted.

Later, when his disciple, the celebrated Magid of Mezritch. had occasion, for the same reason, to intercede with heaven, he would go to the same place in the forest and say: "Master of the Universe, listen! I do not know how to light the fire, but I am still able to say the prayer." And again, the miracle would be accomplished.

Still later, Rabbi Moshe-Leib of Sasov, in order to save his people once more, would go into the forest and say: "I do not know how to light the fire, I do not know the prayer, but I know the place and this must be sufficient." Once more God produced a miracle to save the Jews.

Then it fell to Rabbi Israel of Rizhyn to overcome misfortune. Sitting in his armchair, his head in his hands, he spoke to God: "I am unable to light the fire and I do not know the prayer; I cannot even find the place in the forest. All I can do is to tell the story, and this must be sufficient." And it was sufficient.[8]

God made man because he loves stories.

SUGGESTED READING

If you would like to get more involved in the "story" part of religion of the story, you couldn't do better than some of the following:

Buber, Martin. *Tales of the Hasidim.* New York: Schocken Books, 1961. There are two books by this title: "Early Masters" and "Later Masters." Both are glorious collections of the best of the masters of religious storytelling, the Hasidic rabbis. Ethical and mystical passion at its height.

---

* A story, of course. I make no apologies for using so many Jewish stories in a chapter on Christian ethics. It is surely possible that eighteenth and nineteenth century Jews and first century Christians knew something about the ways of God that twentieth century Christians have somehow overlooked!

Bell, Martin. *The Way of the Wolf.* New York: The Seabury Press, 1969. Reading Bell (or listening to him on the record of the same name) is an overwhelming experience. He (successfully, I think) attempts to re-create the gospel message in new images, using animals and young people.

————. *Nenshu and the Tiger.* New York: The Seabury Press, 1975. More gospel messages in new images.

Carroll, James. *Wonder and Worship.* New York: Newman Press, 1970. A collection of some of the best of Carroll's fairy tales for Christian worship. Delightful. The themes explored in this book range from "The Community of Love" to "Revelation of Death."

Keen, Sam. *Apology for Wonder.* New York: Harper & Row, 1969. A Dionysian theology centered upon the reality of Christ and wonder. Not a collection of stories, but a careful underpinning of the religion of story.

————. *To A Dancing God.* New York: Harper & Row, 1970. A collection of things, with much attention to the art of telling stories.

Kopp, Sheldon B. Guru. *Metaphors from a Psychotherapist.* Palo Alto, Cal.: Science and Behavior Books, 1971. Kopp uses "healing metaphors" from Judaism, Christianity, Winnie-the-Pooh, and almost everywhere else to illuminate the pilgrimage of therapist and patient. A powerful and lovely book.

————. *If You Meet the Buddha on the Road, Kill Him!.* Palo Alto, Cal.: Science and Behavior Books, 1972. In many ways a continuation of the previous book, though with closer attention paid to several 'Pilgrimage Tales" (*Siddhartha, Macbeth, The Inferno, Pilgrim's Progress,* etc.).

Wiesel, Elie. *The Gates of the Forest,* trans. F. Frenaye. New York: Holt, Rinehart & Winston, 1966. Deals with the Hasidism by focusing on the lives of many of the greatest masters.

The Holy Bible, especially the Gospels of Matthew, Mark, and Luke.

Worship and the World

A short time ago I decided to get organized by filing my old sermons. There it was: ten years of words. Mixed in with some helpful moments were large doses of unmitigated boredom and presumption. The filing process was a humbling experience, to say the least.

"The Feeding of the Five Thousand" took the prize for the most preached-about theme. I had tried eight separate times to unravel the mysteries of that story. One time I had focused on the element of the miraculous; other times the shepherd feeding his flock, the Lord's Supper, and the beauty of the young boy's simple offering of his brown bag lunch to the disciples.

Each time I had boldly attempted to get into the heart of the story. But in retrospect, each time I missed what, for the gospel writers, was the most important point of the story—the setting. As a help to understanding the story I offer the following:

SHORT BIBLE QUIZ

QUESTION: *What event does the Feeding of the Five Thousand follow?*

Hint Number 1: It follows a very crucial point in the life of Jesus.

Hint Number 2: That event was probably the most shattering moment in Jesus' life.

ANSWER: Jesus has just been told that John the Baptist had been murdered in a most cruel and sadistic way.

The Feeding of the Five Thousand occurred at a moment when Jesus was shocked, confused, and probably terrified. John, the person Jesus had most admired, the person most closely tied to his own mission and purpose, had been slaughtered by Herod.

Matthew, Mark, and Luke disagree about a number of things,

especially about what follows what in the gospel story—but with *this* story they are very precise. The Feeding of the Five Thousand follows right after Jesus hears of John's beheading.[1]

Just as Jesus' ministry was beginning to make an impact on the world—tragedy of the worst kind. While he was beginning to build some momentum in his work, word had come that his childhood friend and chief supporter had been murdered. So it is not hard to imagine what must have been going through Jesus' mind after hearing the awful news of his friend:

> Fear—Death had knocked on John's door; his own death was coming.

> Immediacy—Time was now short; everything was even more urgent.

> Grief—Plain, simple grief, with all its feelings of being lost, being hurt, and being very, very alone in the world.

With all this on his mind, Jesus had tried to get away by himself to put it all together—to put himself back together. He had tried to get away from people for that desperately needed time for himself.

But there was the crowd, waiting. And Jesus was drawn to them—even at this most confusing and grief-filled hour—both to heal and to feed. And heal and feed he did. From what I read, he fed the crowd in humility and simplicity, and only then did he leave for that all-important time to himself. How beautiful! And even more beautiful because it was, in a way, uncharacteristic of Jesus.

Earlier, when pressured by his mother, he was impatient with her. Later, when pressured by the disciples, he was impatient with them. But here, surrounded by incredible pressures of the worst kind—internal pressures—Jesus responded in simple kindness and generosity. Healing and feeding.

As we move beyond this simple and understated story to reach for its deeper meaning we run into several pitfalls. For instance, we miss the point of the story if we focus on the miracle: "Look at that great miracle Jesus did with those loaves and the fishes!" That's not the point.

At its deepest level, what happened at the Feeding of the Five Thousand is what happens in our time together as a worshiping community:

> God the Father,
> pausing in the middle of a frantic day;

with trouble in Southeast Asia,
trouble in the Middle East and the Far East,
with panic in the ghetto,
and desperation in the suburbs,
with people dying and being born,
finding themselves and losing their way . . .

In all this he is present in loving attention,
here (as my children say, in the center of Rochester,
New York,
United States of America,
Western Hemisphere,
Planet Earth).

The Feeding of the Five Thousand is a simple and most beautiful story. And we only lose that beauty if we focus our attention away from Jesus the person to Jesus the Miracle Worker.

Also, for the sake of the story, I hope there is no moral here —though I can think of a couple of good ones: "No matter how bad off you are, there is always someone worse off." "Other people always come first." These two morals, in particular, cause far more guilt than liberation. And, unhappily for those who take them seriously, they tend to drive people crazy!

It wasn't for the miracle or for the moral that during the first century this story was passed down from family to family until it was finally included within the gospels of Matthew, Mark, and Luke. Rather, in this event above all others, we are left with a unique picture of the person of Jesus affirming the power of life in the face of death.

Celebrating life in the midst of death—that is one of the things the Christian faith is all about. And with a good eye for the spirit, we can recognize this same thing all around us, whether it is Daniel Berrigan in handcuffs, smiling and flashing the peace sign, or someone else praying and trusting in what seems an impossible personal situation. Affirming life in the presence of death.

In the spring of 1972, through very complicated circumstances, I found myself testifying before a grand jury* which was investigating the events surrounding massive police brutality at a peace march in downtown Rochester. The police tactical unit had gone wild, attacking and beating peaceable marchers, shoppers, people waiting for the bus—just about everyone in sight—with little or no provocation. I had been beaten badly, though for no apparent reason.

The grand jury was trying to make some sense of all this and was charged with making some concrete suggestions for the future. Some of the questions I was asked:

<blockquote>

Grand Juror:	"Do you think demonstrations are going to accomplish anything?"
T.B.W.:	'No, probably not. Demonstrations are probably not going to accomplish anything. That's not the point. As I see it, if a demonstration has any integrity at all, it is not just a way of saying "No!" It is a way of attempting to affirm life in the midst of death. A demonstration may be an imperfect way of doing that, but that is what is going on."

</blockquote>

* It can happen in the best of families.

<blockquote>

Grand Juror:	"Have you attended many demonstrations, yourself?"
T.B.W.:	"Yes. I try to make at least one a week."
Grand Juror:	"One a week?"
T.B.W.	"Yes, I get together with my friends each week in public to sing songs, re-tell stories that are important to us and, in our own way, to affirm the power of life in the presence of all the pain and suffering within us and around us."
Grand Juror:	"I don't understand."
T.B.W.	"We call it Sunday morning worship."

</blockquote>

While that may not have been a very decorous response to a serious grand jury. what I had to say was said in all seriousness (despite the obvious grin on my face at the moment).

It was serious, because that *is* precisely what we do each Sunday morning as the Christian community. We gather in public to sing songs, to re-tell stories that are important to us and, in our own way, to affirm the power of life in the presence of the overwhelming pain and confusion that surrounds us.

Though we may be imperfect believers (not always sure exactly what Jesus Christ means in our lives), somehow we are convinced that in the stories of his life and in what happens when we gather in his name, we are brought in touch with a power of life much stronger than any of the death which surrounds us.

TWO PRONOUNCEMENTS

Christians who are uneasy with death often end up faking worship. We prefer to ignore death, both in its present and future realities. So we come together for "inspiration," to be spurred on by morals and object lessons—or for "sustenance" (the gasoline pump theory of Holy Communion).[2] Heaven knows we need both sustenance and inspiration, but when they become the focus of our worship, we are accommodating ourselves to the death which surrounds us. It is so easy to become grim realists, compressing visions into the possible and the secure. Grim realists always seem to miss the point of the Feeding of the Five Thousand.

Others prefer uncompromising joy, the latest fad in Christian worship. Balloons replace grim statues, happy songs and joyous banners crowd out all reminders of the difficulty of human life. Middle-class adults singing happy songs and quantifying anything and everything with "Praise the Lord," oblivious to the incredible pain infecting us—what a ludicrous sight. Celebration without seriously facing the fact of death is damned silly.[3]

The happy revolutionaries of the 60s (whose identity was all bound up with saying "*no*")[4] were fascinated with death. Grim realists are frightened by life. Most congregations are willing to go quietly.

So much for pronouncements.

In the Fourth Gospel, John has Jesus reflecting on the meaning of the Feeding of the Five Thousand:

"I am the Bread of Life.
He who comes to me will never be hungry;
He who believes in me will never thirst."

—JOHN 6:35

No miracle. No moral or little object lessons. Something more. He is pointing to something deep at the heart of the universe—something strong enough and powerful enough to accept and to stand over against the reality of death.

Life is not always easy for me. And I assume it is not always easy for anyone else. Troubles surround us. But always, everywhere—just beneath the surface—is the simplicity, the power of God trying to break into our lives. It is always there, always available. And it is what is most real, most durable. Jesus. Bread. The real stuff of life.

It is good that we have the story of the Feeding of the Five Thousand to remind us what our life is all about.

10
The Clergy: Ringmasters or Animal Trainers?

The traditional dress for clergy is black with a large circle or small rectangle of white at the base of the neck. Someone more clever or deranged than myself might attempt to tie many of the Church's troubles to that simple fact of image. There are historical reasons for our "basic black," but they are hard to remember. For me, the most compelling reasons for wearing black come not from church history or hierarchy but from a country and western singer. In a song he often sings at concerts, Johnny Cash says, "Well, you wonder why I always dress in black?"

> The answer is direct and powerful: the black is for the poor and the beaten down, for the sick and for the lonely and the old. . . .

Rainbow colors, says Cash, are for a world not yet come; but until that time does come, up front there ought to be a man in black.

So far, so good. But black clothing also means drabness, somberness and all sorts of things funereal. It is hard for the small patch of white to bear the full image of Christian hope, overwhelmed as it is by that enormous expanse of penitence.

As an exercise in stretching our imagination, I propose spending a few minutes in fantasizing how the Church would be different if the basic dress of the clergy were other than it is. What, for example, would church life or church attendance be if clergy were dressed as:

> Police Officers
> Magicians
> Life Guards
> Quarterbacks

Garbage Collectors
Ticket Takers (for the Carnival or the Turnpike)
Short Order Cooks
College Professors in Academic Gowns
Fire Fighters
Ringmasters
Nurses
Animal Trainers
Spiritual Ascetics
Corporate Executives
Clowns
Army Officers
Prisoners
Judges
Physicians
Avon Ladies

Spend some time playing with each image. And if you have nothing against marking in books, rank them according to your own preferences.

Happy (in some cases) and sad (in others) to say each of these roles/costumes represents real expectations of real people for ordained clergy. And each represents, in a loose way, self-images of "clergy I have known." If job security were absolute, it would be fascinating to wear a different costume each week of the year (animal trainer, police officer, fire fighter, judge, physician, and life guard during Lent, etc.).

However, in view of the ubiquitous identity crisis now upon us, perhaps the clergy predicament is not so unique. Even so, it is essential to the whole life and ministry of the Church to make some sense out of its appointed leadership.[1] But as the two themes, church life and ordained ministry, are so dependent upon one another, it is not easy to know where to begin.

Probably as good a place as any is with Charles Webb's parable of today's confused world, *The Graduate*. Benjamin Braddock has just been graduated from college and is searching for some meaning and purpose to his life. After a constant barrage of respectable advice from his parents, Benjamin tries desperately to get them to understand him:

"Dad," Benjamin said, "for twenty-one years I have been shuffling back and forth between classrooms and libraries. Now you tell me what the hell it's got me."

"A damn fine education."

"Are you kidding me?"

"No."

"You call me educated?"

"I do."

"Well I don't," Benjamin said, sitting down again. "Because if that's what it means to be educated then the hell with it."

"Ben?" his mother said. "What are you talking about."

"I am trying to tell you," Benjamin said, "I'm trying to tell you that I am through with all this."

"All what."

"All this!" he said, holding his arms out beside him. "I don't know what it is but I'm sick of it. I want something else."

"What do you want."

"I don't know."

"Well look, Ben."

"Do you know what I want," Benjamin said, tapping his finger against the table.

"What."

"Simple people. I want simple honest people that can't even read or write their own name. I want to spend the rest of my life with these people."

"Ben."

"Farmers," Benjamin said. "Truck drivers. Ordinary people who don't have big houses. Who don't have swimming pools."

"Ben, you're getting carried away."

"I'm not."

"Ben, you have a romantic idea of this."

"Real people, Dad. If you want the cliche, I am going out to spend the rest of my life with the real people of this world."[2]

There is something of Benjamin Braddock in all of us. In our cellophane-wrapped, rush-rush world where we all spend so much time flirting with the unreal and the second-hand, each of us from time to time attempts to discover what is real and most important in life.

The "real people" Benjamin Braddock is talking about are the people who have not forgotten how to feel—and to feel deeply. The real people are the ones who care—and who are not afraid to dream or to hurt.

Feeling   Caring   Dreaming   Hurting

This is the kind of world the Church is sent into, because this is the world of Jesus Christ. I will never forget the words of a seventy-year-old grandmother, Gert Behanna, when she was speaking to a group of young people about their place in God's world. She said:

> "Whatever you do, don't be a 'goody-goody.' God's got enough goody-goodies. What he needs now are people who are tough, who will care . . . who can feel. So for God's sake, don't be a 'goody-goody.' "

I can honestly think of no better words for someone entering on the life of Christian pilgrimage.

Other words I shall never forget are those of a schoolboy who was asked what he thought God was like. He said that as far as he could make out, "God is the sort of person who is always snooping around to see if anyone is enjoying himself and then trying to stop it."

It is not difficult to imagine the joy, the freedom, and the spirit that must have been squeezed out of that child's life—how unreal he was encouraged to be. But, of course, it happens every day.

Yet more and more we are coming to see the Christian faith not as something imposed upon us from the outside to "make us good" (whatever that means) or to keep us in line, but as a God-given vision of a Spirit-filled world in which Christ is always present—in the midst of life—to be discovered and celebrated. And He is met not by shutting life out, but by embracing it in all its variety and fullness.

This we know: God is always present attempting to break into our lives. He is always there, in every situation: in the creation, the birth of a child; whenever two people meet over coffee; in every handshake or embrace; at every high school dance and every bridge party; in every occasion of suffering or pain. Whenever we are with one another, hoping with one another, crying or loving or laughing with one another, Christ is present. In every attempt we make, however feeble, at reaching out to one another or to ourselves, he is always there—breaking in on our lives, nudging us on toward completeness.

In our worlds of feeling and caring and dreaming and hurting, Christ is always present in power. And our task as Christian pilgrims is just this—learning to celebrate all the moments of Christ's presence with us; whenever we encounter joy, power, judgment, or forgiveness in our lives to say, "That's God" and rejoice with tears of joy or tears of humility and repentance.

The ordained ministry in all this is to enable the rest of us to be the real, open, loving people of God. That is the central reason we set people aside as ordained ministers. We, as part of the people of God, choose and empower them to enable us to be who we are meant to be, and to do those things God wants us to do.

In the Book of Common Prayer ordination service there is a job description for a priest. It speaks of three things:

MESSENGER: One has got to have the training to teach.
WATCHMAN: One has got to have the guts to speak out.
STEWARD: One has got to have the trust of the community
               of God's people to act as Parent at their table.

These are all "enable words."

The ordination service says nothing about being a third gender (neither male nor female, but spiritual). I will never forget the elderly woman who spoke to my wife soon after we had adopted our first child. She said. "What a nice way for a minister to have a baby!" I repeat, the ordination service says nothing about a third gender.

And it says nothing about being a big shot in the Christian community. Jesus came among us as a servant. As a servant: not to stand over the disciples, but to enable them— to enable them to take their places in God's world as feeling, caring, dreaming children. Children open to the movement of the Holy Spirit.

If I were to think of a single word to describe the ordained person, it would be "enable." To enable us to be all we were meant to be; not to stand over us like a wise parent who says "No! No!" to this, that, and the other, but to stand beneath us, supporting us, opening our eyes and hearts to all the wild possibilities which surround us. To enable us to confess and to celebrate, to rejoice and to love, in all the hurt and all the beauty in life.

As I say, if I had to choose a word, it would be "enable." And if I had to think of a person— an example of what it means to be an ordained person in this kind of world we live in—it would be Murray, in Herb Gardner's play, *A Thousand Clowns*.

Murray doesn't sound very religious, but a wise Christian would say that he is really talking about life as it is given to us, and speaking deeply about the things of the spirit.

Because Murray has been a pretty unconventional guardian for his young nephew, a social worker has come to see about taking the boy away. Murray talks about the child's future:

"And he started to make lists this year. Lists of everything: subway stops, underwear, what he's gonna do next week. If somebody doesn't watch out he'll start making lists of what he's gonna do for the next ten years. Hey, suppose they put him in with a whole family of list-makers? He'll learn to know everything before it happens, he'll learn how to be one of the nice dead people. . . .

"I just want him to stay with me till I can be sure he won't turn into Norman Nothing. I want to be sure he'll know when he's chickening out on himself. I want him to get to know exactly the special thing he is or else he won't notice it when it starts to go. I want him to stay awake and know who the phonies are. I want him to know how to holler and put up an argument, I want a little guts to show before I can let him go.

"I want to be sure he sees all the wild possibilities. I want him to know it's worth all the trouble just to give the world a little goosing when you get the chance. And I want him to know the subtle, sneaky, important reason why he was born a human being and not a chair. I will be very sorry to see him go."[3]

I think that says it. In all an ordained person does—administering the sacraments, preaching, counselling, or just being with the people—he or she will be helping us to get to know the special thing we are, making sure we see all the wild possibilities and that we know the subtle, sneaky, important reason why we were born human beings—and not chairs.

Opening up for us the world of the spirit: that's the issue.

11
The Common Transformed

What kind of universe is this place we live in? Do we live among a strange mixture of sticks and stones, chromosomes and bones, leaves and dirt—each alive in a certain way, but each carrying its own meaning? Or is there something really special going on? The question is not always an exciting one for me, except when I am tired or depressed, and am bothered by more basic questions—my own aloneness or helplessness. Alexander King put it the right way: the question is not whether there is life after death, but whether there is life after birth!

For most of us, amid the dry spots there are moments which are meaningful and which seem to open life up for us. Such moments may be marked by a realization of our vulnerability or a sudden sense of our own power or beauty. The point is that when such moments *do* occur, they hint of a universe which is alive and personal in a way we usually overlook. In theological language, Christians speak of the sacramental side of life, when the common is transformed or when we are transformed through the common.

> And they came to Bethsaida. And some people brought to him a blind man, and begged him to touch him. And he took the blind man by the hand, and led him out of the village; and when he had spit on his eyes and laid his hands upon him, he asked him, "Do you see anything?" And he looked up and said, "I see men; but they look like trees, walking." Then again he laid his hands upon his eyes and he looked intently and was restored, and saw everything.

—MARK 8: 22–25

One of the outrageous aspects of the Christian faith is the belief that the miracles of Jesus are not, at least in the usual sense of the word, miracles at all! They are signs of something basic in the universe, focused through one person in time and space. Jesus touches a blind man and through his hands a powerful personal force enters the blind man's body, re-creating lost connections, revitalizing dormant tissue. And the man sees.

What is so miraculous about that? I, who know something about the power of an unexpected embrace in the midst of an awful depression, can sense the reality of sight restored. That's not too difficult. What Jesus does, simply, is to illustrate all the wild possibilities in a world which is not a closed system.

> Earth's crammed with heaven,
> And every common bush afire with God;
> But only he who sees, takes off his shoes,
> The rest sit round it and pluck blackberries,
> And daub their faces unaware . . .[1]

The world is sacramental. It is alive. And nothing is just what it seems. Thus, a kiss is never just four lips in close(est) proximity. With a kiss I can manipulate, I can lie, or I can communicate; I can transmit love, that most precious of all forces alive in the universe. What is crucial for me to understand is that I cannot *create* love with my lips, my heart, my spleen, or any other part of me. As Frederick Buechner so eloquently says:

> . . . notice this: that love is not really one of man's *powers*. Man cannot achieve love, generate love, wield love, as he does his powers of destruction and creation. When I love someone, it is not something I have achieved, but something that is happening through me, something that is happening to me as well as to him. To use the old soap-operate cliche seriously, it is something bigger than both of us, infinitely bigger, because whenever love enters this world, God enters.[2]

To use another, less romantic example, when I spank one of my children I am sometimes aware (shamefully) that I am simply responding from my own anger. At other times I feel I am helping (painfully) to guide and correct. "An outward and visible sign of an inward and spiritual grace?" Perhaps. Though it may not be strictly kosher to suggest that spanking *may* be sacramental, it would be a serious oversight not to consider the possibility.

What, then, is a sacrament? It is hard to say. Turning the question around, what is *not* a sacrament? Again, it is hard to say. The Church has its official sacraments (Baptism, Confirmation, Holy Communion, Penance, Matrimony, Holy Orders, and Unction), and there are innumerable unofficial ones. What is common to all sacraments is that they are moments when the life of God touches us, moments when what lies at the heart of the universe breaks into our own lives.

Perhaps, as a means of digging a little deeper, we might try a quiz:

A QUIZ

Which of the following are sacraments? Or sacramental?
—An embrace.
—Ironing someone else's shirt.
—Cutting down a tree.
—Planting a tree.
—A gift of a handful of jelly beans from a five-year-old.
—A trip through an art museum.
—Coffee hour after church.
—A peace march.
—A gathering in support of a particular war.
—A wedding.
—Bandaging a child's hurt finger.
—Psychiatric counselling.

If your answer to any of the above is "No," what would make that a sacrament? If your answer to any of the above is "Yes," what would make that other than a sacrament?

The personal issue is always whether the universe is really alive with meaning or not. Is life sacramental (in touch with a love and power breaking in upon us) or do we grimly create our own meanings? In locating the source of the "bad side of life," we are fairly generous: "I got up on the wrong side of bed." "There just seems to be nastiness in the air." "I don't know what made me do it." "The devil made me do it."

It is harder for us to get in touch with the sacramental side of life. But there are moments when the light shines through. After bedtime prayers my seven-year-old son asked what "Deliver us from evil" meant. I tried to explain that when we are mean to someone, it is not just we who are mean. There's meanness all over the place and it kind of grabs hold of us. His eyes lit up. And then he said, "I know, Dad. It's like when I get up in the morning. If I get up on the left side of the bed. I'm left out. And when I get up on the right side of the bed, I'm '*Right On!*' "

He's right. There is the "Right On" side of life when we are in touch with the love and creativity of the Maker of the universe. Our problem is to recognize it, to celebrate it, and to integrate

our lives into it. One of the functions of the Church is to help us
do just that, as with bread and wine.

I

To our table we come as a family for our family meal,
to be refreshed, renewed, and filled.
We come as we come to any meal,
hungry and thirsty and at our host's open invitation,
seeking sustenance, life, and the power and strength
to live another day.
One brings the bread.
The bread of wheat from the land of God's own doing,
from the farms of man's own planting,
from the mills of our continual working.
The bread of sharing
which unites all of mankind
under rather uncomfortable terms.
This is the bread of
bread and water for the prisoner who
spends his years
counting the days;
Bread inundated with peanut butter and jelly,
fit only for the strongest and youngest tummy;
Bread, broken into crumbs for the birds by an
aspiring St. Francis;
and bread from the bread line, which is neither
too far in the past
nor too far removed from our present
to remember.
Parker House rolls to bread and water,
crumbs for the bird feeder to bread
yielding mold for the microscope—
the Bread of our sharing,
the one expression of our common humanity.

And lest we forget,
the Bread of our incompleteness.
Bread from wheat protected by subsidies and supports,
Gathered, ground, and baked by strong and
often tired hands,
who have mouths to feed, themselves,
and troubles to bear,
things to think about,
and renewing to get done.

Bread processed by highly organized workers,
a bit suspicious of management,
a little more than suspicious of the new shipment
of brand-new machines for automated baking.
Bread for which people somewhat less affluent than we
will shed blood.
    But our bread is lucky bread,
for it will go into waiting hands
instead of rotting and spoiling over long months,
while thinking of the hungry mouths and
decaying stomachs
of little peasant children who,
for the price of a one-way fare aboard a steamer
or a small piece of foreign policy,
would be eating bread.
    And so, gathered from our common life
is the bread of sharing
and the bread of brokenness—
of our inabilities and suspicions—
our incompleteness.
One brings Bread,
gathered from the pantry shelf,
from a long forgotten storage bin,
from the prisoner's cell
to our common table.

    Another, somewhat ambiguously, brings
                            wine to the table.
Ambiguously, because it graces other tables as well:
makeshift tables of cardboard cartons on the Bowery,
finely linened tables of solid oak
graced with crystal candlestack holders.
We bring an ambiguous bottle of wine,
reflecting our joy and misery
gathered in a finite space.
    Wine from the grape,
gathered from punch bowls at the Marriage Feast,
from the sherry glass toasting new-found success,
from the hip flask of celebrating some new
                          depths of despair,
from very ordinary cups of ordinary people
who have nothing else to drink.
    Quite ambiguously, joy—despair—
                      celebration—degradation,
and a most peculiar glow
are gathered into one provision for the meal.

Wheat-Grapes
Bread-Wine
Strength and Joy
Daily Bread and Festive Wine
Empty Stomachs and Joyless Hearts
are all gathered into a finite space in very finite forms,
and offered to the common host
who will feed his common guests
at a very uncommon meal of bread and wine.

II

    Still another has his gift to bring.
This other, host or family,
host and family,
no one present can claim him strictly as his own,
comes himself to the Master's table.
"Think not that I have come to bring peace,"
he said,
"But rather I have come with a sword."
And so he has.
I remember when he used that sword like a scalpel
on the Family,
stripping them all of that very precious thing
we call self-respect.
This was not the kindly thing to do, but he used it
more than once to cut away almost all
                      of what was Everyman.
You should have seen him peeling away layer after layer,
until we could hardly recognize the Everyman
                      we had formed.
It seemed cruel.
You would have said so if you had seen it.
He used it to cut deep down inside.
Layer after layer of
everything his mother had wanted him to be,
everything he had a right to be
everything he had an inclination to be,
the scalpel cut away.

Then, the protest: "Is nothing sacred?"
To which the other replied, "Certainly not this."
And all the while he cut away, he kept insisting
he was after something
that was gasping,

choking for air,
or dying.

Again, the protest: "Now you're getting personal."
But the other continued to cut away,
replying to his unwilling victim
that he had only scratched the surface
(in really personal terms).

Then a lot of things started flying:
conventional standards,
prejudicial banners,
social graces,
small talk's traces,
even Everyman's precious standing in the community,
until everything was gone,
except for something none of us had really
                                    expected to find.

What was left
was choking for air,
an empty space waiting to be filled;
anyway, something really peculiar,
reaching, stretching for life,
as if it actually hoped or dreamed or yearned.
It's really hard for us to say
just what it was.
At first the sword had looked awfully menacing,
to those, that is, who had not been cut into.

And there was something else about this other
(among many other things).
It was what he did
with what he found
after all the cutting.
"I came that they might have life," he said,
"More abundant life."
And that's the way it seems.
He would take this little gasping, choking
thing he found
and put everything he had in it.
It was hardly like artificial respiration:
that anyone can do with
pushing and pulling,
urging and coercing,
and giving good advice.

It was hardly like artificial respiration—
more like transfusion,
which is a pretty costly process.
At least it would be for me.
Because the needle hurts
and I feel pretty weak afterwards—
and that's only blood.
    But he would take this little, weak, almost
whimpering, gasping, choking thing
and pour into it everything he had to give:
health,
a divine kind of madness,
power,
and the common necessities of life.
He seemed to have these only to give away.
Cut, slash, and cut.
Give, pour out, and give.
Feed, feed, and feed.
He went about this in an almost frantic way,
(though, of course, taking time out for
proper refreshment and renewal of himself).
But as time went on
he found he couldn't give enough of himself,
for there were many people,
so many people,
there were so many, many people
that there was no other way to feed them all
except by becoming Bread and Wine.
Wheat-Grapes
Bread-Wine
Strength and Joy
Daily Bread and Festive Wine
Empty Stomachs and Joyless Hearts
Fullness—despair—celebration and degradation
are all gathered into finite space in finite forms
on the Table.
And so we come to the Master's Table,
offering ourselves to the sword which alone
can reveal our hunger;
offering the fruit of our own labor—
our own aspirations and degradations—
our own Bread and Wine,
that in them
and through them
he might give us that precious gift
of Himself.

12
Crucifying the World: The Heart of Our Pilgrimage

How would you like to crucify the world? Really crucify it? Hang it up on a cross and let it die. I am sure there have been times when everyone of us has felt like that—crucifying the world. And somehow, each of us has felt that way for the same basic reason: the world is crazy. Really crazy.

And it is not "interesting crazy," like "Look at that crazy outfit he is wearing." But sick crazy. The world *is* sick and it makes people sick.

Take the kind of competitiveness in which we live, where there is nearly always a winner . . . and nearly always a loser. That's not very difficult to see. If you think about it, "Survival of the Fittest" almost always ends up meaning "Survival of the Least Human." This, in a world filled with beings who are struggling to become human.

I think of Everyman, who is on the make to provide the "best" for his family—and ends up away from home three to five nights a week. And when he is home, he is so full of tension that his family falls apart. But he is determined to have "the best."

This whole cycle happens nearly every week, in nearly every family. There are a lot of words for this whole thing. The most adequate is probably "crazy."

The world is really hard on someone who does not play its crazy games. In the midwest, the young college girl who does not get accepted by the sorority of her parents' choice feels crucified. Of course, we say, she will get over it. But there are many, too many, who do not. Who never do.

Any student who has flirted with the notion of suicide as the only way out can tell you how crazy the world really is. He or she knows intensely the incredible pressures, the *unbelievable* pressures to get the grade, to get ahead, to get yourself in the same awful box your parents are already in.

Pity the young man who does not buy into this—and instead spends his time wandering around looking for something other than grades or a well-paying job in the near future. We tell him something's *wrong* with him and then pack him off to the school counselor, a psychiatrist, or the Army recruiter. They'll give him the *proper* kind of motivation and direction he needs to get along. Get along with whom?

What difference does it make—what *real* difference does it make if I get to be president of my organization or make all B's? What *real* difference? But the system seeks to have us all locked in—all locked up.

What I am really trying to say is that the world is extremely cruel and punishing toward anyone who does not play by its rules —however noble or insane those rules are. St. Paul called it crucifixion. When he chose to stop playing crazy games, he said, "I have been crucified to the world." And I think each of us, in our own ways, has some idea about what he meant.

Think back to the young family man, who in the name of doing everything possible for his family is in fact doing everything that will cause it to fall apart—working nearly every night, so full of tension that he cannot give anything to his family. How is it possible to break out of all that? It is almost as if something big, something really big must happen to shake him loose from all of that—from all the sickness and the craziness of the world.

Centuries ago, off in what seemed like an unimportant corner of the world, such an event, such a confrontation did take place. And it had all the simplicity and all the power anyone could ask. What was said and what was done laid bare our predicament and our choice.

Bless are the rich,
    for they shall rule the earth.

Blessed are the poor, for theirs
    is the kingdom of heaven.

Blessed are the calm and
    collected, for little can touch
    them.

Blessed are those who mourn,
    for they shall be comforted.

Blessed are the aggressive,
    for they shall be promoted.

Blessed are the meek, for they
    shall inherit the earth.

Blessed are those with finesse,
    for in avoiding controversy
    they shall come out ahead.

Blessed are those who hunger and
    thirst for righteousness,
    for they shall be satisfied.

Blessed are the cool and callous,
    for they shall emerge
    untroubled.

Blessed are the merciful,
    for they shall obtain mercy.

Blessed are the manipulators, for they shall achieve power.	Blessed are the pure in heart, for they shall see God.
Blessed are the patriots, for they shall make the country strong.	Blessed are the peacemakers, for they shall be called sons of God.
Blessed are the nice people, for all will speak well of them.	Blessed are those who are persecuted for righteousness' sake, for theirs is the kingdom of heaven.

The words of Jesus were hard words, cutting words, threatening words. To make them comforting or reassuring is to mock them.

In our world where diligence is rewarded, his Parable of the Laborers in the Vineyard was revolutionary. (Matt. 20:1–16) In our world, where moral respectability is taken very seriously, Jesus' treatment of the young adultress (caught in the act) was disgusting. (John 8:2–11) In our world of carefully hedged loyalties and responsibilities, the Parable of the Good Samaritan was an outrage—latter day Sunday School interpretation aside. (Luke 10:25–37)

It's bad enough to believe stragglers are entitled to the same good things as the rest of us. And undoubtedly worse to use a national enemy as an example of what it means to be a good neighbor. But the story of his treatment of the adultress, what effect might *that* have on the national morals? What incredible courage it must have taken to stand there and say, with a straight face, that the Holy One, the Mighty God believed such utter nonsense!

DIAGNOSIS: Crazy.
PRESCRIPTION: Treat as an enemy of the people.

So there stood Jesus: meek, poor, hungry. thirsty.
And there stood Pilate and all the others: rich, cool, patriotic, anxious for promotion and the good will of the people.

As there was no easy compromise, they led Jesus out of the city and nailed him to a tall wooden cross. And killed him. After flimsy accusations by his enemies, a trial with no defense, brutality by his captors, he went quietly to his death.

This all happened in a way difficult to explain—or fully understand. What happened there (whips, thorns, nails and spear) must have been a horrifying thing. And what happened was also beautiful—the most beautiful thing ever to have happened on this planet.

It was beautiful—for at that moment one person accepted the

full cost of being human . . . really human. At that moment, in such a way that there would never be any question about it, one person utterly and completely rejected the craziness of the world. And there is a remarkable beauty in that.

They killed him. They murdered him, because he wouldn't play by the crazy rules we all set up.

And he could have escaped. He could have escaped; and died of old age, pneumonia, or exhaustion at some later date—if only he had promised to be a little less human. If he had acted with a finer air of respectability (spending less time with *those* people), he could have, he really could have lived a longer life.

But by accepting his death he told them in the only complete way there is to say such things: "You're asking me to be crazy, too! To play by small rules created by small people to keep their world small and manageable. And that kind of life is really not worth the price. Survival of the least human is no survival at all!"

And so he crucified the world—and the world crucified him right back. And that was where it all began—returning the world to sanity and some health.

Listen to the power of the words of the man who saw it all so clearly, who felt it all so deeply—the words of a free man:

"Far be it from me to glory except in the cross of our Lord Jesus Christ, by which the world has been crucified to me, and I to the world. For neither circumcision counts for anything nor uncircumcision, but a new creation. Peace and mercy be upon all who walk by this rule, upon the Israel of God. Henceforth let no man trouble me; for I bear in my body the marks of Jesus. The grace of our Lord Jesus Christ be with your spirit, brethren. Amen."

—GAL. 6:14–18

And that, in a few words, is where it's at. If you want to understand the Christian faith at its deepest and most powerful level, that is where you begin—and that is where you will end.

Out of all the turmoil and all the confusion over the uprising at the Attica prison, there is one thing I will not forget. It was one of the Black prisoners, standing before the TV cameras, trying to express what the whole event was meaning to him. I do not remember his name, but I do remember his words: "If they won't allow us to *live* like human beings, at least we will *die* like *men*."

There is a lot about Attica that I do not understand—and I am sure that white middle-class people like me will be the last to know the "facts" of the matter. But I do understand what that one prisoner was saying: "If they won't allow us to *live* like human beings, at least we will *die* like *men*."

Or in the words of another time, another place: "Father, if it is at all possible, let this cup pass from my lips. . . ."

To be a man, to be a woman, to be a free and together people in this crazy world costs something. We know that. That much is clear. Heroism and courage are words no longer reserved for warriors and statesmen. The great struggle is where you and I live out our lives—where the issues are more subtle and more demanding. To be a Christian—to be in Christ—is both a terrifying and a glorious thing, and certainly not to be taken lightly. It is what salvation is all about.

> "Survival of the least human . . . "
> *Lord have mercy.*
> "I only want the best for my family . . . "
> *Christ have mercy.*
> To be a man or a woman in this crazy world.
> *Lord have mercy.*

A strange fact: When God became human, he did not come to us as a Sunday School teacher, a police officer, or as the president of his organization. He was just a man—"just" a man. Is that really so hard to understand?

And when he died, there were no parades, no wreaths, no eulogies. But he died as a man—just a man, a free man. And it was beautiful.

Notes

Chapter 2.

1. J.D. Salinger, *The Catcher in the Rye,* (Boston: Little, Brown & Company, 1951), p. 91.

Chapter 3.

1. Bernard Gunther, SENSE RELAXATION *Below Your Mind,* (New York: Collier Books, 1968), p. 56.
2. *Ibid.*
3. Soren Kierkegaard, *Works of Love,* in *A Kierkegaard* Anthology, edited by Robert Bretall (Princeton: Princeton University Press, 1951), p. 289.

Chapter 4.

1. James Broughton, "The Last Word," in *Religious Drama 3*, (Cleveland: Meridian Books, The World Publishing Company, 1959).
2. A.J. Langguth, *Jesus Christs,* (New York: Harper & Row, 1968), pp. 38-9.
3. Jacques Ellul, *The Presence of the Kingdom* (New York: The Seabury Press, 1967), p. 9.
4. *Ibid.,* p. 11.

Chapter 7.

1. Rowland Cox, unpublished manuscript.
2. Sidney Carter, "The Lord of the Dance," © copyright 1963 by Galliard Ltd. All rights reserved. Used by permission of Galaxy Music Corp., N.Y., sole U.S. agent.

Chapter 8.

1. Frederick Buechner, *Wishful Thinking: A Theological ABC,* (New York: Harper & Row, 1973), pp. 50ff.
2. In precise terms, "The truth of ethical relativism lies in the moral law's inability to give commandments which are unambiguous, both in their general form and in their concrete application. Every moral law is abstract in relation to the unique and totally concrete situation. . . . If formulated in commandments [law] never reaches the here and now of a particular decision."

Paul Tillich, *Systematic Theology, Vol. III,* (Chicago: University of Chicago Press, 1963), p. 47.

3. Again, in the words of Paul Tillich, "Its motivating power is limited and. . .it cannot bring about a full reunion with what we ought to be." *Ibid.,* p. 49.

4. Dietrich Bonhoeffer, *The Cost of Discipleship,* (New York: Macmillan, 1959), p. 120.

5. It should be noted that in John's gospel, there is a special usage of "sign," quite different from the notion of rule or law. John understands certain events (Feeding of the Multitude, The Marriage Feast at Cana, The Raising of Lazarus) as symbolic of a deeper truth, and calls them "signs." For him, in those events, timeless realities are made real and present *in* time. For John, the universe is alive and exciting; as C.H. Dodd notes, "He writes in terms of a world in which phenomena—things and events—are a living and moving image of the eternal, and not a veil of illusion to hide it, a world in which the Word is made flesh." C.H. Dodd, *The Interpretation of the Fourth Gospel,* (Cambridge: Cambridge University Press, 1960), p. 143.

6. Sheldon B. Kopp, *If You Meet the Buddha on the Road, Kill Him!* (Palo Alto, Cal.: Science and Behavior Books, Inc., 1972), p. 4.

7. Paul Reps, ed., *Zen Flesh, Zen Bones: A Collection of Zen and Pre-Zen Writings,* (Garden City, N.Y.: Doubleday & Co., 1961), p. 62.

8. Elie Wiesel, *The Gates of the Forest,* trans. F. Frenaye, (New York: Holt, Rinehart & Winston, 1966), introductory notes.

Chapter 9.

1. The Gospel of John is quite another matter. John's purposes are different from the other gospels and he omits the story of the Baptizer's beheading entirely.

2. In times past the analogy was a popular one. The minister is a gasoline station attendant who weekly fills the tanks of churchgoing Christians with heavenly fuel, so, as the saying goes, they "can make it through the week."

3. Nothing is more shattering than to read a Mary Corita-type celebrative book while you are depressed.

4. I will never forget the words of one of my close friends when the Viet Nam war "ended." He said, with awful anxiety, "With this gone, what am I to do? I don't know who I am any more!"

Chapter 10.

1. The word "appointed" is used advisedly. As will become clear, I trust, the real and crucial leadership of the Church of God is not necessarily clerical. In the first great moments of church life it was not Moses who functioned as priest, but Aaron. For a powerful

and sensitive treatment of the matter, see Ahad Ha'am's chapter on Moses in *Nationalism and the Jewish Ethic,* (New York: Schocken Books, 1962). The dialectic both between priest and community and between priest and the prophetic force within God's people as dealt with by Ha'am is as helpful for the Christian community as it is for the Jewish.
2. Charles Webb, *The Graduate,* (New York: The New American Library, Inc., 1963), pp. 33-34.
3. Herb Gardner, *A Thousand Clowns,* Copyright 1961, 1962 by Herb Gardner and Irwin A. Cantor, Trustee.

Chapter 11.

1. Elizabeth Barrett Browning, "Aurora Leigh," Book VII.
2. Frederick Buechner, *The Magnificent Defeat,* (New York: The Seabury Press, 1968), p. 34.